COMPUTERS AND MUSICAL STYLE

THE COMPUTER MUSIC AND DIGITAL AUDIO SERIES
John Strawn, *Series Editor*

Volume 1
DIGITAL AUDIO SIGNAL PROCESSING
Edited by John Strawn

With contributions by J. W. Gordon, F. R. Moore, J. A. Moorer, T. L. Petersen, J. O. Smith, and J. Strawn

Volume 2
COMPOSERS AND THE COMPUTER
Edited by Curtis Roads

With contributions by or about H. Brün, J. Chowning, J. Dashow, C. Dodge, P. Hamlin, G. Lewis, T. Machover, J.-C. Risset, C. Roads, and I. Xenakis

Volume 3
DIGITAL AUDIO ENGINEERING
Edited by John Strawn

With contributions by J. McGill, F. R. Moore, J. A. Moorer, P. Samson, and R. Talambiras

Volume 4
COMPUTER APPLICATIONS IN MUSIC: A BIBLIOGRAPHY
Edited by Deta S. Davis

Volume 5
THE COMPACT DISC: A HANDBOOK OF THEORY AND USE
Ken C. Pohlmann

Volume 6
COMPUTERS AND MUSICAL STYLE
David Cope

VOLUME 6   THE COMPUTER MUSIC AND DIGITAL AUDIO SERIES

COMPUTERS AND MUSICAL STYLE

David Cope

A-R Editions, Inc.

Madison, Wisconsin

Library of Congress
Cataloging-in-Publication Data

Cope, David
    Computers and musical style / David Cope.
        p.   cm. — (The Computer music and digital
    audio series; v. 6)
    Includes bibliographical references and index.
    ISBN 0-89579-256-7 (hardcover)
    1. Style, Musical—Computer programs.
    2. Computer composition.   3. LISP (Computer
    program language)   I. Title.   II. Series.
    MT723.C68   1991
    781.3'453—dc20   91-11494
                                                        CIP
                                                        MN

A-R Editions, Inc.
801 Deming Way
Madison, Wisconsin 53717-1903
(608) 836-9000

10 9 8 7 6 5 4 3 2 1

Dedicated to
Keith Muscutt and John Strawn,
whose expertise and advice
contributed greatly
to the preparation
of this book.

CONTENTS

. . . .

A NOTE
ABOUT THIS SERIES

. . . .

The Computer Music and Digital Audio Series was established in 1985 to serve as a central source for books dealing with computer music, digital audio, and related subjects. During the past few decades, computer music and digital audio have developed as closely related fields that draw from a wide variety of disciplines: audio engineering, computer science, digital signal processing and hardware, psychology (especially perception), physics, and of course all aspects of music.

The series includes, but is not limited to, works in the following forms:

- textbooks at the undergraduate and graduate levels;
- guides for audio engineers and studio musicians;
- how-to books (such as collections of patches for synthesis);
- anthologies;
- reference works and monographs;
- books for home computer users and synthesizer players.

As for content, the series addresses audiences from a wide variety of disciplines. Also, the series addresses both beginners and experienced practitioners in the field. Therefore, it is not suprising that some material in the series or even within a given volume will seem too advanced or too elementary for a given reader. But by including material for all levels and all types of readers, the series serves as a source of introductory material as well as a unified reference collection.

In this volume David Cope presents a composer's tool—a computer program that can accurately represent and freely manipulate musical styles.

The composer enters musical data into the computer; the program creates new musical material. To be sure, a program such as this can aid a composer in creating new compositions. But the value of Cope's research goes beyond this practical application.

Historically, analyzing printed scores and generating compositions automatically by computer were among the first areas of research when computer programmers tackled music. These research projects arose at about the same time when computers were first used for directly generating sound, which has drawn more public and commerical attention.

There are actually two problems to be solved. First, how can stylistic elements of historical and contemporary composers be accurately captured? More important, how can differences between distinctive styles be handled easily by one system? In the early days, the rules programmed into computers for generating works in a given genre or style were cumbersome. The resulting musical works were rarely compelling. Changing from one style to another often required reprogramming from scratch. David Cope has solved many of these problems.

A further contribution is that Cope's system provides a lens through which we can examine musical style in a new light (the "signatures" discussed in this book) and thereby learn more about style itself. By strict musicological criteria, the musical examples that his system produces do not accurately match the originals. But the musical results are convincing enough that this work now deserves to reach a broader audience, through means such as this volume.

How can one measure the effectiveness of work in this area? One measure of a successful synthesis technique is its ability to replicate sounds of traditional instruments. Yet another is its ability to create sounds from more than one instrument family. The flexibility with which the composer can manipulate sound is also important. By way of analogy, Cope's work is successful in simulating many aspects of compositions in various styles. The *EMI Brahms* is as distinct from *EMI Bach* as the real Brahms is distinct from the real Bach. Cope's system even captures styles outside the European tradition, and it allows for exploration of changes in style. Ultimately, the most convincing argument for the effectiveness of Cope's work is to listen to the music itself. We have freely reproduced score segments and even entire movements. I encourage the reader to play these through.

This book uses ideas and terminology from music and computer science. The cross-fertilization that results from applying technology to the arts is sometimes confusing. To give one example: The word *function* has a distinctive definition in each field and is used with both meanings even within one chapter here.

Finding a single audience for an interdisciplinary work such as this is difficult. Throughout, we assume the ability to read and understand music;

Cope's argument will be hard to follow for those without some musical training. But not everyone who can read music knows computer programming. Therefore, the LISP code essential to understanding the core of Cope's work is introduced very gradually.

The interdisciplinary challenges to the reader underline the advantage of the cross-fertilization between technology and the arts. Each learns from the other; both are thereby enriched. I hope that David Cope's book will be a springboard for deep and fruitful discussions in both areas.

John Strawn
Series Editor

PREFACE

. . . .

In 1981, during a moment of recklessness, I wrote the following in a daily journal:

> I envision a time in which new works will be convincingly composed in the styles of composers long dead. These will be commonplace and, while never as good as the originals, they will be exciting, entertaining and interesting. Musicians and non-musicians alike will interplay with programs which allow them to endlessly tinker with the styles of the composing programs. I see this as a parallel to the synthesis of, say, piano sounds, where synthesis and sampling devices can convincingly recreate the timbre of an instrument. In the former case, however, it will be the *order* of the sounds and the algorithmic processing of that order that will be paramount. I see none of this as problematic. Machines, after all, only add and subtract. Programs that benefit from those operations are only as good as their creators.

This book describes many aspects of a program I have since devised for the replication of musical styles. These aspects include a non-linear (not composed beginning-to-end) and top-down compositional approach and an intricate rules-based expert system defined according to experience gained in my twenty-three years of teaching music theory. While all of the aspects considered in this book are critical to the success of the overall program, the crux of style imitation lies in the development of a musical pattern matcher and the inclusion of an ATN (augmented transition network) compositional approach.

I have felt for years that I recognize composers' styles by subconsciously matching motives of various types from work to work (I make no contention that mine is anything but my own personal experience). These motives may be orchestration techniques, use of certain meters, or, more likely, sequences of pitches and rhythms. While these motives are never exactly the same, enough is there for me to hear what I call "signatures."

If there is a discovery here, it is that one way of defining style is through pattern recognition and that musical style can be imitated if one can find what constitutes musical patterns. Further, comparisons of these patterns from work to work will reveal those patterns that are generic to a composer's style and those that are found in a single work only.

While I developed this approach on my own, the concept itself is hardly new. Superimposing representations of two or more things to discover how they are similar or different is a straightforward principle. Yet, sometimes the application of rudimentary ideas in just the right manner and to just the right degree can produce novel results.

I am also not the first to recognize the potential for ATNs to be productive in the re-creative process of musical composition. While the actual system presented here may be the first realization of musical ATN, the concept is not mine. Relating nouns and verbs to tonics and dominants, though not a common form of analysis, has been something theoreticians have discussed previously. While none to my knowledge have built actual systems using these principles, this situation is not due to any lack of suggestions in the literature.

I mention these two points in order to ask the reader to be aware that looking for special secrets within the covers of this book will be disappointing. There is no magic in my work, only long hard hours of programming, a lot of musical experience, and some lucky guesswork at certain junctures. This may be a function of the programming language I use. William Kornfeld wrote (1980, p. 6): "It is impossible to list the features of LISP. LISP has very few of them."

Reviewers often find the musical results of the programs I've developed interesting, even ground breaking. Yet they are often critical of my writing about it because, I believe, they expect the formula, the great insight that will show them the light. If there is such a potion, and I gravely suspect there is none, it is the unglamorous musical combination of the pattern matcher and the ATN generator.

OVERVIEW

Chapter 1 of this book presents a brief history of automated music and especially emphasizes musical style. The first part includes brief descriptions of various computer music projects. It shows how early attempts to codify and replicate musical style demonstrated potential; but only recently, with advanced hardware, more memory, faster speeds, and MIDI (for listening quickly to output), have results proved successful. The second part looks at a few programs in detail. The final section of Chapter 1 introduces the author's own project, Experiments in Musical Intelligence (EMI), one major focus of this book.

Chapter 2 deals with defining the basic concepts and parameters of musical style. This is followed by the basic concepts of functional harmonic tonality (expectation-fulfillment-deception) as they relate to the programs presented later in the text. This section also touches on the hierarchical model derived by Heinrich Schenker. Germination of form and non-linear composition are discussed in the next section. Top-down approaches take precedence: Sections are derived from movements, phrases from sections, motives from phrases, and notes from motives.

Texture and timbre are then discussed. Harmonic grammars, as a result of straightforward contrapuntal simultaneity, are also explored. This is followed by a discussion of the basic concepts of linguistic representations. These generally take the forms of rules and values. Parsing provides understanding of written languages, and Chapter 2 demonstrates its potential for parallels in music. Transformational concepts are also discussed in this section, and examples are included. This is followed by a description of augmented transition network (ATN) parsing, which occupies the central focus of the last section of Chapter 2. Of the many grammar types, only ATN allows the recursive possibilities inherent in LISP and is thus the approach of choice.

Chapter 3 covers LISP (short for list processing) and its application to the analysis of musical style. The basic concept of defining an idea and then working toward actual manipulation of data is covered in this section. LISP functions are defined according to standard lambda binding to arguments along with variables, conditionals, and standard programming techniques. Function definition is presented along with the advantages of data abstraction. Straightforward and readable examples of LISP functions in terms of music are also provided. LISP has existed in many different dialects for decades. An attempt to standardize a single form has resulted in the creation of COMMON LISP. This is the form of LISP used in this book. All of the functions described herein should run in any COMMON LISP implementation without revision.

Chapter 4 presents the specifics of a small invention-composing program based on the concepts presented in previous chapters. The route from inception to surface incarnation (a top-down approach) is shown. Prototypical (completely machine-composed) musical fragments demonstrate how the program has a computational logic based on linguistics and includes dictionaries and rules for ensuring nonarbitrary gestures.

Chapter 5 begins by describing the complexities of programming the keyboard style of J. S. Bach and closely follows two examples by EMI. The next section discusses the differences between the creation of an invention and composition by EMI in more complex forms. This is followed by a description of the machine composition of a Mozart sonata in three movements. Then follow examples of a machine-composed Joplin rag and a slow movement of a sonata in the style of Prokofiev. Non-Western musical styles are the focus of the next section in this chapter. The music of Bali is the subject of replication. Counterpoint and further examples complete this chapter.

Chapter 6 demonstrates computer-assisted composition. EMI offers a variety of interrupts and insertion nodes that allow users to have as much access to the process of composition as they desire. Choices range from automaton— in which the computer composes the entire piece—to complete composer control, with many gradations between. Once defined and characterized in a dictionary, a style may be injected into a work in any proportion. Hence, new styles can be created by interlocking two or more dictionaries. Two recent hybrid works from EMI are discussed in detail from the compositional point of view and in the context of the linguistic–musical style model. Also presented are algorithms that reflect the process of original composition.

CONCLUSION

Strategies are compositional choices made within the possibilities established by the rules of style. For any specific style there is a finite number of rules, but there is an indefinite number of possible strategies for realizing or instantiating such rules. And for any set of rules there are probably innumerable strategies that have never been instantiated. For this reason it seems doubtful that styles are ever literally exhausted, as they are sometimes said to be. (Meyer 1989, p. 20)

I am a composer seduced into programming. I've heard all of the real Mozart sonatas many times. What a treat to hear one I'd never heard before! I hope the readers of this book will find the same kind of interest in this project as I do: intrigue, joy, and a bit of fright. After all, no matter what your take on musical style imitation, remember that the machines have had great teachers—the works of the great masters themselves.

ACKNOWLEDGMENTS

I would like to thank the following individuals, who have generously given of their time and energy in the preparation of this book. Keith Muscutt, as the dedication indicates, helped greatly not only in the preparation of this manuscript but in the nurturing of EMI as well. The work *For Keith,* discussed in Chapter 6, is also dedicated to him. The other dedication goes to series editor John Strawn, without whose sage advice and experience this book would not exist at all. Faculty colleague Linda Burman-Hall has constantly provided new challenges and inspiration for EMI. Her support and faith in the project have been instrumental in any success it has earned. Then there is Betty Freeman, whose invitation for an EMI concert at her house first provoked the question of style combinations. Her warm support of a controversial project of this nature has been very helpful (hence the dedication to her of the *Freeman Quartet* of Chapter 6).

I would also like to thank the following individuals for their continued support during the building of EMI: Eli Blevis, David Jones, Gordon Mumma, Paul Rinzler, and my wife and family, who have put up with me for all of these years. A special acknowledgment goes to Bob Giges, whose video *Bach Lives! At David Cope's House* (available from him at Porter College, University of California at Santa Cruz, Santa Cruz, CA 95064) has been a great source of recurring inspiration during times of self-doubt.

David Cope

BIBLIOGRAPHY

Kornfeld, William. "Machine Tongues VII." *Computer Music Journal* 4,2 (Summer 1980): 6–12.

Meyer, Leonard. *Style and Music*. Philadelphia: University of Pennsylvania Press, 1989.

A BRIEF BACKGROUND OF AUTOMATED MUSIC COMPOSITION

. . . .

INTRODUCTION

Before describing my own work, it would be useful to review some of the other events and discoveries that have preceded it. This will place my own research in context and allow readers the opportunity to measure its relative significance.

A brief history of automated music composition could extend back to the carillons of the medieval era or before. Barrel organs, player pianos, and music boxes could also be included. However, such developments should be considered related to performance; that is, the outcome of their mechanical output is for the most part predictable. For the purposes of this book, only those instruments, machines, or programs that create new works qualify for inclusion. These are "automata" capable of creating original music.

HARDWARE

Among the most ancient "hardware" of composing instruments, aeolian harps and wind chimes tenuously fall into the category of "composers" since the outcome of their performance, in both cases, depends on the direction and amount of wind that nature provides unpredictably. Wind or aeolian bells have for centuries been a part of many world cultures. *Gunte* is the Hindu term for bells, and they are found adorning the temple roofs of many villages in India and Tibet. This is also true for China (Edgerly 1942), where they are called *feng-ling*. In Japan they are the *furin*, and in Burma the *khew* hang from temple and cave roofs alike.

Despite the fact that today aeolian harps are observed as musical novelties, there have been periods when their production and use have been prolific. King David's *kinnor*, a wind-played lyre, supposedly sang at night from the force of the north wind (Marcuse 1975). Saint Dunstan (d. 988) was suspected of sorcery for having experimented with a "harp" that played of its own accord when hung in the breeze (Buchner 1959). Giovanni Battista Porta's *Magiae naturalis* discussed the aeolian harp as a serious musical instrument capable of wonderful sonorities and unexpected sounds (Porta 1558). Athanasius Kircher (around 1650) designed elaborate wind-performed instruments (Kircher 1646; Buchner 1959).

The eighteenth-century English poet James Thompson discussed the aeolian harp, and the "ghostly sound of chords" became a part of the lore. Samuel Johnson (1700–1748) wrote in *Castle of Indolence*: "The God of Winds drew Sounds of deep Delight: Whence, with just Cause, The Harp of Aeolus it hight. Ah me! what Hand can touch the Strings so fine?" G. C. Gattoni of Como, Italy, created his *armonica meteorologica* in 1785. This huge instrument, also called the *arpa gigantesca*, had fifteen metal strings, which Gattoni strung between his house and a nearby tower. The strings, vibrated by the wind, supposedly forecast the weather as well as created interesting sounds. In the eighteenth and nineteenth centuries the French celebrated the *harpe d'eole*, their version of the aeolian harp. These and other references are discussed in detail in Marcuse (1975).

The aeolian harp enjoyed special popularity in Europe during the Romantic period, particularly with builders like Longman and Broderip, William Jones, and Clementi and Company in England and Heinrich Christoph Koch and Friedrich Kaufmann in Germany (Buchner 1959). Kaufmann, of Dresden, was one of the most famous builders of musical automata. An entire book (Kastner 1856) was devoted to the construction and care of aeolian harps.

Variations of aeolian harps have been numerous through the ages. The aeolian bow is such a case. Aeolian bows are typically constructed with horsehair or rattan attached to bamboo, much as in traditional string instrument bows. These then hum at different pitches. The instrument is suspended from trees in Indonesia, swung from a performer's hand in Indonesia, Malaysia, and West Africa, and attached to kites in China, Korea, Japan, Thailand, and certain parts of Indonesia. Some historians also claim that musical arrows were at one time popular in China (Edgerly 1942). These were tubular arrows that sang while flying through the air.

In Bali, there is the *pinchakan*, a bamboo rattle operated by the wind, and the *bulu parinda*, large aeolian pipes hung from the tops of trees. There is also the tradition of placing bamboo tubes along irrigation channels of terraced rice paddies so they would, when full, tip over and knock against a rock. The sound of each tube would be tuned to a different pitch of a scale so the farmer could immediately locate a blocked irrigation channel by noticing an absent pitch in the scale. In Japan, the "deer scarer" is a bamboo hydraulic, tipping when full and, according to tradition, scaring the deer away. The use of bells on domestic herds of sheep and cattle is ubiquitous.

The pealing of bells, known throughout Europe during the Gothic and post-Gothic eras, also represents an example of automatic composition. Special bells, rung by campanologists pulling ropes, create unpredictable melodies based on gravity's effects on the bells' swinging motions. Titles of songs such as "Eight-Splice Surprise Major" (Schafer 1973) indicate the nature of the results of the "calling of changes" during performance.

Other unusual automatic instruments include the gilded brass ball, a sealed ball that when rolled created ever different music (described by Bonanni 1722), and the *sundari* of Bali, an impressive aeolian flute that works in the rice fields (see McPhee 1966). More recently, modern fountain chimes, large hydraulic instruments created by many instrument builders including Bernard and François Baschet as well as Ward Hartenstein, create new and varied music.

One of the first hints of machine composition came from mathematician Ada Lovelace around 1840. Her colleague Charles Babbage had invented a "calculating engine," now considered to be the precursor of the modern-day computer, and she wrote: "Supposing, for instance, that the fundamental relations of pitched sound in the signs of harmony and of musical composition were susceptible of such expression and adaptations, the engine might compose elaborate and scientific pieces of music of any degree of complexity or extent" (Bowles 1970, p. 4).

Communications expert Elisha Gray invented the "musical telegraph" in 1874. This single-octave keyboard device produced arbitrary music during telegraph communications as a by-product of Morse code letter representations. Each key was attached to a single-tone "transmitter," which used spring-loaded metal reeds to transform electricity into sound. Interestingly, the device was polyphonic and anticipated telegraph multiplexers (which transmit more than one signal simultaneously over a single wire).

One player piano composer does deserve mention in the category of mechanical performance of formalized music: Conlon Nancarrow. Since the late 1940s, he has "composed" a series of *Studies for Player Piano,* many of which are the result of strict applications of mathematical formulae (Cope 1989b). Many of those numbered in the thirties and forties take the form of strict canonic realizations of mathematic proportions. These are performed on one of his two player pianos in his Mexico City home. Hence, there is a mechanical performance of a mechanically composed work: an integrated musical automaton.

Mathematician Joseph Schillinger, whose major books (1948; 1978) brought forth great controversy, developed schemata for composition of new works by machines. His Rhythmicon (which was built by Leon Theremin and composed and performed rhythmic patterns) and Musamaton (his name for automatic instruments that varied extant music) were examples of his often complex mathematical theories, which were nonetheless intended for the musically uninitiated.

Chance music, championed by John Cage and others since the early 1950s, especially when paired with the use of machines, is worthy of mention here. Cage's *Reunion* (completed in 1968), for example, is a work performed (most notably) by Cage and Marcel Duchamp by playing chess. The sounds were triggered for release to loudspeakers by special photoelectric switches located in the chessboard. Cage's *Cartridge Music* (completed in 1960) is another example of the rigorous application of a formalism, in this case a score consisting of random overlays of various sheets with abstract lines, circles, and dots (Cope 1989b). The translations of these "scores" by performers using phonograph cartridges attached to amplifiers represents a kind of automata. So does Charles Dodge's *Earth's Magnetic Field* (completed in 1970), in which the computer musically translates indices of change in the magnetic field of earth.

Steve Reich's *Pendulum Music* (completed in 1968) is another example of automatic music hardware. The work requires that microphones be attached to the ends of long cables, which are in turn plugged into amplifier–loudspeaker systems. The microphones are then hung from the ceiling of the performance area, all at the same distance from the floor, and directly above their associated speaker. They are set into motion when performers pull back the cables and release them in unison. As the microphones pass by their respective speakers, feedback is generated. This begins as short bursts and then lengthens as the microphone pendulums lose energy.

During the performance, the performers join the audience in watching and listening to the work. Their only remaining duty is to unplug the amplifiers in unison when the feedback becomes continuous.

Pauline Oliveros's *I of IV* (completed in 1966) uses two tape recorders and a single tape loop to create double feedback. The complex arrangement creates reverberation in thick layers that continuously fold over one another. Even though one can control the entering sound, the looping system is so complex as to be completely unpredictable in its manipulation of that sound. Many of Oliveros's works, particularly from the 1960s and 1970s, exist only in the form of diagrams of machines or machine arrangements. Many other composers, such as Allen Strange (*The Music of Dod*, completed in 1977), Gordon Mumma (*Hornpipe*, completed in 1967) and David Behrman (*On the Other Ocean*, completed in 1977), among others, have created original machines that play seriously active roles in the compositional process with their inventors (Cope 1989b).

Brian Eno has created many different devices that play and create automatically. He says: "Since I have always preferred making plans to executing them, I have gravitated towards situations and systems that, once set into operation, could create music with little or no intervention on my part. That is to say, I tend towards the roles of planner and programmer, and then become an audience to the results" (Holmes 1985, p. 143). Many of his works are machines or machine setups themselves. Often, situations are created where a kind of ambient music will continue indefinitely, all created by the circumstance set in motion by Eno but then out of his control.

Obviously, automatic music composition is best suited to the modern-day computer and the synthesizers they can control. For the most part, however, composers and programmers have tended toward the study of pitch (tuning systems), timbre, and space rather than toward the actual computer ordering of sounds as in composition. Certainly the creation of new machines specifically designed as composers of music has not been at the forefront of new designs of, say, computer-controlled synthesizers. Most work has instead resulted in software.

SOFTWARE

The "software" of early automatic music may have originated with Pythagoras (circa 500 B.C.), who believed that music and mathematics were not separate studies; an understanding of one was thought to lead directly to the understanding of the other. He was the first known philosopher to propose a theory of a "music of the cosmos." He believed that the same mathematical laws governed the motions of heavenly bodies of astronomy and the system of musical intervals he had discovered. Plato agreed with Pythagoras's views and, in the *Republic* (X, 617), gave birth to the myth of the "music of the spheres," in which, as Hippolytos has it, "Pythagoras maintained that the universe sings and is constructed in accordance with harmony; and he was the first to reduce the motions of the seven heavenly bodies to rhythm and song" (Murchie 1961, p. 67). Both Plato and Pythagoras, however, took great liberty with their theories, and they remain today more poetic than concrete.

Johannes Kepler's "music of the spheres" (Kepler 1619) represents a good example of music *formally* derived from non-human sources. Basing his results on various transpositions of the (then) known planetary orbits, Kepler calculated six new melodies, one of which was Earth: endless repetitions of "mi, fa, mi." Saturn (see Figure 1.1) was a short and low pattern. While Kepler's results fall far short of aesthetically pleasing music, his belief in a universal harmony has continued to make an impact through the centuries. It is his approach—the "automatic" production of music—that is still of interest.

Gareth Loy (1989) points out the history of "formalisms," such as Guido d'Arezzo's (eleventh century) production of musical lines from texts, and identifies these formalisms as precursors of automatic music composition. He also notes that fifteenth-century composers employed isorhythms and isomelos, rhythmic and pitch structures of different lengths, in creating their motets. Likewise, the acrostic use of the letters in names for notes (as in BACH, the German notation for Bb–A–C–B♮) is a way of composing automatically. While these are all relevant to some degree, the rigor of automata is not seriously approached.

One of the first composing machines to produce actual results, built by H. F. Olson and H. Belar in 1951, consisted of two random-number generators and a sound-generating system. Pitch and rhythm were controlled by weighted probabilities during the composition process. Sawtooth wave outputs completed the device, which predated standard synthesizers by many years. Some of Olson and Belar's first attempts involved biasing the machine toward the style of Stephen Foster melodies through first-, second-, and third-order frequency counts.

Most of the early work in automated music composition, however, was accomplished by Lejaren Hiller in collaboration with Leonard Isaacson (Hiller and Isaacson 1959). Hiller's work led to programs written on the Illiac computer and the composition of the *Illiac Suite for String Quartet* in 1956. His program applied rules to lists of random numbers, with the results printed in standard notation. The music ranged from monophonic

FIGURE 1.1 Music for Saturn from Kepler's *Harmonices mundi libri V*, 1619.

and four-part first-species counterpoint to highly random chromatic structures. Figure 1.2 describes Experiments Two and Three of the four produced. Figure 1.3 gives the last four bars of the "random chromatic music" of Experiment Three.

In the mid-1950s, Iannis Xenakis (1985) began working on mathematical techniques and developed computer programs based on these processes. Works such as *Metastasis* (completed in 1954), *Pithoprakta* (completed in 1956), and *Achoripsis* (completed in 1957) were based on numeric calculations. Since his works centered on mathematical models, they were often composed by machines. His writings (particularly *Formalized Music,* 1971) are standard references for work relating to the early developments of computer composition. He has used probability laws, stochastics (a mathematical theory that develops predictability from laws of probability), game theory, and Markov chains (left-to-right chains of events in which new events are determined by the outcome of the choice of its immediate predecessor) as formalized processes for composition. Xenakis's music typically contains thick textures with many diverse elements sounding at once. Sometimes, as in *Metastasis*, where the textures result from glissandi, techniques are limited to one or two effects. More often, however, his computer programs will produce variations with extreme contrasts.

Other experiments during this time included computer generation of hymn tunes based on the statistical analyses of thirty-seven hymns. These analyses were carried out by F. Brooks, A. Hopkins, P. Neumann, and W. Wright (Hiller 1970). Their work required that some similarity be imposed on each of the computer-generated tunes, such as that they all be in C major, share a common meter, and end on a dotted half note. The process included the generation of random integers, screening these integers according to predetermined probabilities, and then running recursive procedures for those integers requiring rewriting.

Robert Baker's *CSX-1 Study* (completed in 1958) employed the MUSI-COMP (short for music simulator interpreter for compositional procedures) program at the University of Illinois. Baker and Hiller then collaborated in the creation of *Computer Cantata*. Completed in 1963, this

Experiment Two: Four-part first-species counterpoint

Counterpoint rules were added successively to random white-note music as follows:

a) Random white-note music
b) Skip-stepwise rule; no more than one successive repeat
c) Opening C chord; cantus firmus begins and ends on C; cadence on C;
   B–F tritone only in VII chord;
   tritone resolves to C–E
d) Octave-range rule
e) Consonant harmonies only except for 6/4 chord
f) Dissonant melodic intervals (seconds, sevenths, tritones) forbidden
g) No parallel unisons, octaves, fifths
h) No parallel fourths, no 6/4 chords, no repeat of climax in highest voice

Experiment Three: Experimental music

Rhythm, dynamics, playing instructions, and simple chromatic writing

a) Basic rhythm, dynamics, and playing-instructions code
b) Random chromatic music
c) Random chromatic music combined with modified rhythm, dynamics, and
   playing-instructions code
d) Chromatic music controlled by an octave-range rule, a tritone-resolution
   rule, and a skip-stepwise rule
e) Controlled chromatic music combined with modified rhythm, dynamics,
   and playing-instructions code
f) Interval rows, tone rows, and restricted tone rows

FIGURE 1.2 Experiments Two and Three of the machine-composed *Illiac Suite for String Quartet.*

highly serialized composition employs various tempered tuning systems (from nine to fifteen notes per octave) and is one of the more important pioneering works of automated composition. The development of MUSI-COMP and the subsequent DARMS (digital-alternate representation of musical scores) at the University of Illinois made it one of the centers for research in computer-generated music during the art's formative years.

In 1963 Herbert Brün completed *Sonoriferous Loops* (for instrumental ensemble and tape) using MUSICOMP. This work and his *Non-Sequitur VI* (completed in 1966 for tape and ensemble) are based on various probability distributions entered as data into the computer. James Tenney's work at Bell Laboratories produced a number of important works involving computer composition, including *Four Stochastic Studies* (completed in 1962), *Stochastic String Quartet* (completed in 1963), and *Dialogue* (completed in 1963).

Around 1960, Pierre Barbaud (in collaboration with Roger Blanchard— see Ames 1987) developed concepts of algorithmic composition working

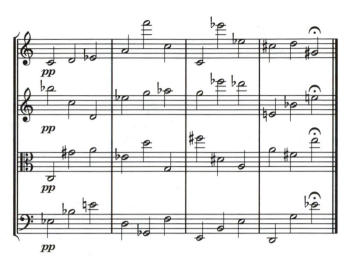

FIGURE I.3 The final four bars of the "random chromatic music" of Experiment Three of the *Illiac Suite for String Quartet.*

primarily with permutations of traditional tonal harmonies and twelve-tone processes of random selection. During the next ten years Barbaud worked to develop aesthetics that championed automated music composition (Barbaud 1966). Barbaud and Blanchard's experiments produced an orchestral work called *Imprévisibles nouveautés-Algorithme I.*

John Myhill's *Scherzo a Tre Voce* (completed in 1965) utilized machine-chosen and drawn-melodic contours to create an electronically produced score. Myhill's background in mathematics and philosophy led him to create some of the earliest writings on the relationship of machines and music cognition (Myhill 1979).

The use of computers to analyze musical style, aside from those already mentioned, began to gather momentum in the mid- to late 1960s (Brook 1969). These include Arthur Mendel and Lewis Lockwood's Princeton Project (Lockwood 1970). Their work covered the *musica ficta* of (particularly) Josquin des Prez (1440–1521). Jan LaRue used computer techniques at New York University to describe stylistic characteristics of eighteenth-century symphonies (LaRue 1967). He was able, for example, to discover low pattern redundancy rates in the music of Joseph Haydn. Allen Forte (1967) of Yale University has also used computers for style research, particularly in areas related to music theory (notably set theory). Edmund Bowles writes prophetically:

One obvious result of such work is a more systematic and objective approach to the analysis of musical style, or content. The computer forces more rigor on the workways of the scholar, at the same time providing the means for larger and thus more reliable data sampling. One has the feeling that computerized content analysis will lead slowly to a more satisfactory answer as to what *style* really is, at least in its quantitative sense. (Bowles 1970, p. 19)

Most style analysis during this period depended on statistical distributions of various musical parameters. W. Fucks (1962) reported observing first-order skip distributions (frequency versus pitch interval between successive notes) that correlated exactly with the common practice period (1600 to 1900) and not in music before or after the time. Not too surprisingly, his graphs for Bach and Beethoven correlated almost exactly with the norm, while those for Webern did not. C. Bean (1961) made first-order frequency counts of sonatas by Mozart, Beethoven, Paul Hindemith, and Alban Berg, with the first three composers showing the most commonality. Bean treated each note, regardless of duration, as a single entry in his count to produce rates of information transformation.

The work of Nicholas Ruwet (see Roads 1985a) is particularly interesting in its relation of music and language. His more recent analysis (Ruwet 1975) follows top-down processes and uses the approach that in order to establish the correctness of a theory one should attempt to falsify it. Using this technique, broad ideas are first proposed and then tested for their validity rather than accumulating narrow ideas to create broad ones. Ruwet, a linguist, has gone so far as to propose generative grammars for the creation of new music. He also promulgates the concept that actual sound must be studied as well as the representation of sound in a score.

J.-J. Nattiez's (1975) work is based on semiotics in music. He believes that signs may be used in generative processes. He argues against, however, the use of transformational theory, as espoused by Noam Chomsky, and disagrees with many notions paralleling Schenker's (1933) theories and those of Chomsky (1965).

James Gabura used computer analysis to make style comparisons, particularly with the music of Haydn, Mozart, and Beethoven. He found, for example, that Haydn's harmonies move faster than those of Mozart or Beethoven. Gabura's study and that of Robert Baker proved amazingly close, even in large samples (Gabura 1965; Lidov and Gabura 1973; see also Lefkoff 1967 and Broeckx and Landrieu 1972). Styles of non-Western music were researched at the University of California at Los Angeles under the leadership of Mantle Hood. Fredric Lieberman's (1970) computer study of Javanese *gamelan* music mentions the need for future study of pattern recognition in the study of musical styles.

Composition using stochastic procedures continued during this period without regard for studies of musical style. Gottfried Michael Koenig's

Project 2 (completed in 1969; see Roads 1985b), composed with the use of non-stylistically based statistical procedures at the Institute of Sonology in Utrecht in the Netherlands, is a significant example of automated music composition of the late 1960s. His *Übung für Klavier* (completed in 1970) also uses these procedures effectively.

GROOVE (general real-time operations on voltage-controlled equipment; see Mathews and Moore 1970) was created by Max Mathews and Richard Moore in 1968. It provided Laurie Spiegel, among others, with opportunities for exploration of partially automated composition. Her *Patchwork* (completed in 1974) displays intriguing real-time aspects of computer-assisted composition. "The program I wrote had all Bach's favorite manipulations—retrograde, inversion, augmentation, diminution, transposition—available on switches, knobs, pushbuttons and keys so that I could manipulate the 4 simple melodic and 4 rhythmic patterns with them in the same way that a player of an instrument manipulates individual tones" (Spiegel, Laurie. Liner notes to *The Expanding Universe*. Philo Records, No. 9003, 1980).

John Cage and Lejaren Hiller's dynamic *HPSCHD* (completed in 1969) was composed by a MUSICOMP subroutine called ICHING, which generates numbers from 1 to 64. The work, whose title is an abbreviation for "harpsichord," consists of algorithms that choose left- and right-hand passages from works by Mozart and other composers (Cage 1968). Computer-produced lists of random numbers also define loudness and treble/bass control for playback.

POD is an interactive or computer-assisted composition program developed by Barry Truax during 1972–73 at the Institute of Sonology, Utrecht, and later at the Department of Communication Studies at Simon Fraser University in Burnaby, Canada. It consists of a number of sub-programs that are used for interactive composition and that utilize real-time synthesis. The compositional model employed includes "sound object selection," "syntactic field specification," "distribution algorithms," and "performance variables," with the user attempting to establish a relationship between the first two levels so that the "semantic level of operation is that of users evaluating interim results and modifying the strategy for obtaining a satisfactory goal structure" (Truax 1977). Variations of POD (including POD4, POD5, POD6, and PODX) have introduced solutions to problems of real-time operation and full-scale interactivity. POD is most successful in its ability to be used by composers having diverse styles. It accomplishes this goal by implementing levels of control applying to structural characteristics of statistical distributions of sound. It allows one to define the role and significance that initial strategies will have on resulting compositions. Heavy doses of constraints produce fairly predictable results, while simple protocols result in surprises.

Among others using composing grammars is Curtis Roads, whose TREE and COTREE programs were developed from formal language theory (1985a). TREE is a grammar-specification language for music, and COTREE is an actual composing language. Roads has explained the programs this way:

> Compositional expressions coded in COTREE are compiled into a score using the grammar specified with TREE. Both languages use a context-free grammar augmented by control procedures. As an extension of the sequential languages used in formal language theory, the notion of parallel rewrite rules is introduced in order to specify musically concurrent events. (Roads 1985a, pp. 426–7)

Mapping from abstract syntactic forms generated by COTREE into lexicons of sound objects is also possible.

David Levitt (1984) developed a jazz improviser program that included harmonic, melodic, and thematic constraints and produced solos from chord progressions. His program relied heavily on the normalization of musical lines to harmonic consonance.

Charles Ames developed Cybernetic Composer for stylistic imitation of various popular music types such as jazz, Latin jazz, and rock. Using a MIDI interface, his program performs new compositions faithful to the conventions of these styles. Ames also uses machines for composition in other ways, both statistical and algorithmic, and his programs have created works like *Concurrence* (for solo violin; completed in 1986) and *Protocol* (for solo piano). Ames's more recent Compose program (completed in 1989) allows users to work with a variety of mathematical and linguistic techniques including what he terms "Chomsky Sequences," "Mandelbrot Chaos," "Markov Chains," and "Poisson Distributions" (among others).

MORE RECENT PROGRAMS

With Cybernetic Composer and EMI (the subject of later chapters), automated music composition has begun to develop analogs to musical style. As can be seen by the numerous references to *stochastic* and *random* in the foregoing description of the formative years of automated music composition, its foundations often rested in music bereft of recognizable style.

In contrast to this, consider the work of Otto Laske, who has been one of the major proponents of musical intelligence as related to computers and cybernetics over the past few years (Laske 1973). He sums up his current views when he states:

> The question is: How can we transfer human musical expertise to a computer and represent it within the machine? How can we construct musical knowledge bases incrementally? How can we get the machine to explain its musical reasoning to a human being? There is nothing peculiar about musical expertise that would force us to use different methods from those used in artificial intelligence applications today to solve these very legitimate problems. (Roads 1986)

Laske describes KEITH as a rule system that makes music-analytical discoveries. He takes the view that a music analysis processor should develop at least three representations of music: "what is heard" (sonological representation), "what is understood" (music-analytical representation), and "what is said" (linguistic or music-theoretical representation). He considers each of these stages as a computational component of the analytical system, with each in turn the product of a sequential subset of those stages. The first component, for example, consists of five separate levels. The second computational component is a recursive control structure determining the sequence of tasks pursued by the processor. It consists of an agenda, an interpreter, and a set of heuristic rules. The third computational component is less defined than the first two but includes representations of instantiated concepts, an utterance builder, a sentence and paragraph builder, an analysis editor, and the ultimate theory of the analyzed work(s). This results in the form of a printed verbal accounting of the program's understanding of the work under analysis. To date, KEITH stands as a concept rather than a fulfilled program; the author states that it "would require several man-years" to complete it. However, the approach is thorough and realizable, and its ultimate implementation could prove quite valuable for the front end of a musical style generator.

There is a composing "program," currently commercially available (see Mozart listing in the Bibliography), based on a sixty-four bar "musical dice game" (*Musikalisches Würfelspiel*), which is generally attributed to Mozart (K. Anh. 294d, 1787), although some question his authorship. Johann P. Kirnberger and Joseph Haydn, among others, also constructed such musical parlor games. This eighteenth-century practice is called *ars combinatoria* (combinatorial art—see Ratner 1970 and 1980). Interestingly, D. A. Caplin first experimented with the *Musikalisches Würfelspiel* in the mid-1950s in a program written for the Ferranti Mark computer.

Hiller (1970) notes that this ranks it as among the earlier attempts at computer composition. Mozart is the name of the latest version of the program (Meier 1984). The music in Mozart is organized in independent two-bar sub-phrases marked A, B, C, D, E, or F as in Figure 1.4a (Mozart's original had accompaniment as well). The monophonic two-bar sub-phrases can be arranged in any manner. This is accomplished by throwing a die. Each number on the die is assigned to one of the two-bar sub-phrases; throwing a number selects the associated sub-phrase. Another throw of the die chooses one of the remaining sub-phrases, and the process continues until all six sub-phrases have been arranged. Any selection of the given measures will produce a viable combination.

Figure 1.4b is a newly composed version (form: A C D B F E) that I created using a die. The range of the new organization works effectively (no connective leaps larger than a fifth) and follows typical tonal constraints. Figure 1.4c is less satisfactory (form: E A D C F B). Here the opening seems more of an ending and is quite contrary to tradition. Interestingly, the sequence of bars 3–4 and bars 5–6 is very musical. In Figure 1.4d, the rearrangement is more effective (form: B D F A C E) but still unbalanced according to interval connections (i.e., the abnormally wide leap between the end of bar 6 and bar 7).

This rather simple program, while performed mostly for amusement, presents some interesting principles that, if more elegantly addressed, could serve as the basis for a moderately effective composing program such as that used by John Cage and Lejaren Hiller in the creation of their composition *HPSCHD*. One foregone conclusion of any program built along these lines is the knowledge that arrangement of a composer's work will surely result in an alteration of some of the elements of that composer's style.

Another commercially available program combines elements of different works in order to achieve new possibilities. Conceived by Yaakov Kirschen (1989) and called Music Creator, this software stores the chords, melodies (pitch), and rhythms of familiar works. Three works, X, Y, and Z, are chosen. "Composing" in essence involves applying Z's rhythm, for example, to Y's melody, and this combination is then draped over X's chords. Other permutations of these variables are possible. The program transposes the melody if necessary to fit with the new harmonies. If one chooses the same work for all three variables, the work is unaffected by the process and the output is the same as the input. Because the composition is explicit (i.e., nothing random in the process), the same choices always create exactly the same results. Different permutations of the same variables, however, produce significantly different music. Style occasionally survives the process, though more typically it is lost amid the sudden changes that occur.

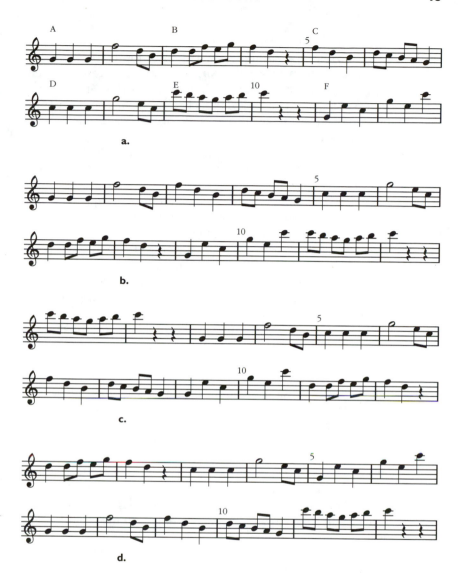

FIGURE 1.4 The melody of Mozart's *Musikalisches Würfelspiel* (a) and three correct new versions of it (b–d).

The Music Creator software seems most interesting when mixing musical styles. Choosing, for example, works by Chopin, Bach, and a contemporary rock group may produce surprisingly musical results. When successful, the program blends the music into new styles. At its worst, Music Creator "composes" nonsensical pastiches. Of the first commercially available programs, Music Creator is one of the first to deal explicitly with problems of musical style.

Though the principal aim of this book is to cover EMI, a rules-based system, the potential of neural networks (see Dolson 1989; Gjerdingen 1989; and Scarborough, Miller, and Jones 1989) must at least be addressed. Neural networks, often called parallel distributed processing or connectionist modeling, may be defined as non-linear hardware or programs that reinforce and diminish connections among internal nodes by how successfully they contribute to matches of recursively fed data. By sweeping (often hundreds of times) through a neural net, a set of data (which could be musical representations) is "learned." While this is a simple explanation of a very complex phenomenon, it does make the important point that neural nets operate somewhat differently than (or as extensions of) constraint-method programming. Current research suggests that with enough melodies a net might, for example, replicate new works in the style of learned music.

Jamshed Bharucha has proposed a connectionist model of harmony where "each event in a musical sequence activates tone units and activation spreads via connecting links to parent chord units and then to parent key units" (Bharucha 1987, p. 1). Peter Todd has developed networks that create new melodies out of what he terms "composition by plan manipulation" (Todd 1988 and 1989). This involves the network producing new tone sequences based on perceived regularities in previously learned sequences. Performance considerations of neural nets are the focus of Barry Vercoe and Marvin Minsky's work at MIT's Media Laboratory. Here, learned accompaniments follow every nuance of tempo indicated by human performers connected to the net via contact microphones.

The future of musical neural nets appears bright as of this writing. While little actual music has been produced, and that which has is simplistic and generally uninteresting, the connectionist concept is elegant and especially suited to music as concrete musical data can so easily be represented by linear number sequences.

Employing more linear aspects of computer technology, Kemal Ebcioğlu (1987) used predicate calculus to develop some 350 rules governing the voice-leading requirements of Bach chorales. The harmonizations have great similarity to those of Bach but (obviously) without the convincing exceptions to the rule. Ebcioğlu's program employs "backtracking," a process that allows for voices facing deadends to retrace their steps and make alternate choices for more correct alignments with their counterparts (see also Schottstaedt 1989).

Tommaso Bolognesi works principally with automatic composition involving self-similar music. His algorithms generate a variety of spectra from regulated fractals (based on Benoit Mandelbrot's studies—see Dodge and Bahn 1986) to noise and polyphonic Lévy-Flight music (multidimensional random motions in acoustic space). His work also incorporates a variety of somewhat elegant stochastics designed purposefully to avoid embedding any kind of formalized musical grammar in the compositional process. While obviously very different from my research that follows in this chapter, Bolognesi's work, with its attendant factor of noise, holds interest for those interested in forced computational accidents (Bolognesi 1983).

S. R. Holtzman uses a Generative Grammar Definition Language (GGDL) to describe unambiguous and formal rules for music composition. His program uses Chomsky rewrite rules (0–3) and a hierarchical set of rules that operate at macro-, micro- and note levels. A composer using the GGDL approach becomes a selector of material rather than its generator: "Designs may also be checked for logical (i.e., functional) consistency. In music, efficiency is not a primary criterion for design or composition. Nor can the correctness of the logic of a musical language be objectively evaluated. In music there is no right or wrong. Some music just sounds better" (Holtzman 1981, p. 63).

Marc Leman's approach to the cognitive study of music relies heavily on symbolic/subsymbolic processing and DHN systems (Dynamic Hierarchical Networks). This latter approach can be identified as a listener's experience of non-verbal units (of some kind) correlated with this listener's state of musical knowledge prior to the experience. DHN systems are also self-adaptive and thus provide an attractive way to develop fully independent replicative programs. Leman's is an adaptive rather than separatist approach. Rules and intuitive deduction networks need not act independently but in concert. The rules network models itself on the actual processing of the human brain, and the intuitive deduction network concentrates on how the human brain processes. Leman does not consider the differences between them to be trivial (Leman 1989).

Fred Lerdahl and Ray Jackendoff (1983) make a strong case for a deep parallel between music and language. In particular, they postulate the importance of "time-span reduction" (pitch hierarchy) and "prosodic structure" (temporal importance of pitch and harmony). Their theories are not wholly innovative, borrowing from Schenker ("prolongation") in music and Chomsky ("transformational grammar") in linguistics. However, the manner in which they credibly relate their research to the musical experience on the one hand and cognitive science on the other provides a formidable framework for understanding the analyses they present and for further research.

Stephen Smoliar's (1980) work with computer analysis of music using the hierarchical techniques of Heinrich Schenker is particularly relevant to the use of transformational grammars in music. His work develops techniques for computer-assisted analysis, particularly of tonal music. His statistical approach to style analysis, though only briefly explored in print, appears useful and pertinent to both traditional and contemporary music theory.

The history of automated music composition deserves far more than the space allotted here. The reader is encouraged to pursue further research through readings provided in the bibliography (see especially Lincoln 1970; Ames 1987; and Loy 1989 for overviews).

AN INTRODUCTION TO EXPERIMENTS IN MUSICAL INTELLIGENCE (EMI)

EMI was conceived in 1981 as the direct result of a composer's block. Feeling I needed a composing partner, I turned to computers for assistance, believing that computational procedures would cure my block. Since random processes did not fit my aesthetic, I also began studying musical style.

In order to accomplish this task, I first built a generator that would follow certain very specific protocol routines in ordering context-free symbols. I used the artificial intelligence language LISP and followed a strictly Classical tonal model. The actual generation initiated hierarchical processes whereby each phrase began as a single symbol (the most important) and then incrementally grew by a fleshing out ("top-down" in computer terminology) of phrase structures. This process, a separate but related issue and hence not discussed here in depth, was termed *nonlinear composition*. In 1985, the work *Out from This Breathing Earth* was completed. The music from this work in Figure 1.5 is chromatic, obviously based on motivic generation of ideas, but lacks coherence and serious evidence of my style.

I next built a dictionary consisting of representations for harmonic chords and melodic notes of Bach. These representations were then reordered into correct but different arrangements. In simple terms, explicit meanings (semantics) were provided to each of the symbols, which were previously limited only by order (syntax). This created an expression or

FIGURE 1.5   First and seventh movements of *Out from This Breathing Earth* by Experiments in Musical Intelligence (EMI).

interpretation of the correctly generated symbols and ultimately rough surface detail (grammar). Enough of the early Baroque qualities of motor-rhythm, part-writing, and so forth, were factored into the process in order to flavor the musical examples. Within a few weeks, the computers at EMI were producing generic compositions of the period. Often convincingly Bach-like, they indicated that the process had worked but that simplistic dictionaries would have to be extended and honed before improved replication could take place.

I then took the identical rules base that had produced believable Baroque music, created a Bartók dictionary, applied it to the rules base, and "generated" a composition. The music that emerged through the sampler at EMI unmistakably displayed the stamp of the Hungarian composer's style. The simple Bartók dictionary, even with the Bach rules base, provided enough information for the parsing device to create convincing replications of Bartók's stylistic genre, if not of his music itself.

FIGURE 1.6   Initial machine-composed examples of J.S. Bach (a), Ludwig van Beethoven (b), Johannes Brahms (c), and Béla Bartók (d).

In 1986, the development of MIDI (Musical Instrument Digital Interface) provided opportunity to code complete works into my computer's memory in a compact and logical manner. By August 1987 I was able to derive short replications of Mozart and other composers. I presented the first works at the International Computer Music Conference at the University of Illinois (Cope 1987a). Figure 1.6 shows the short beginnings of

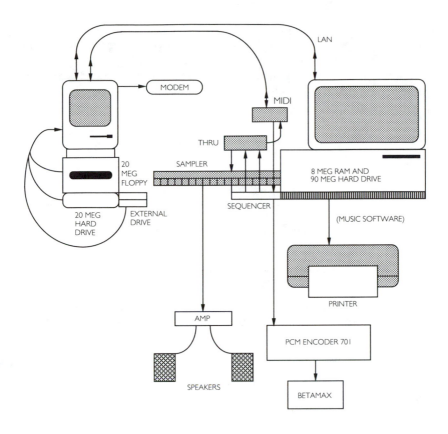

FIGURE 1.7 The EMI Workstation.

these works, which exemplify machine-composed imitations of Bach, Beethoven, Brahms, and Bartók.

Around this time I also began overlaying pattern-matched *images* of works, and EMI completed its first full work in a definable style—a Bach invention. In 1988, the first published magazine articles appeared in *Computer Music Journal* (Cope 1987b) and *AI Expert* (Cope 1988a). EMI then completed a Kyrie in the style of Palestrina and a complete EMI Mozart sonata for solo piano. I have presented this work at various conferences (Cope 1988b; 1989a; and 1990).

The EMI system on which the examples for this book were composed follows the layout as shown in Figure 1.7 (Cope 1991a and 1991b). Two Macintosh computers are required for the operation of the studio. To the right, a Mac II *composes* works. They are then printed out in numeric code or "mailed" through a local area network (LAN) to a Mac Plus, where works are *performed*. I have found that dedicating separate computers to composition or performance has the advantage that input–output (I/O) remains stable. That is, in such a system it is never necessary to switch connections or rearrange ports. The sampler (my choice over synthesizers since they produce "real" sounds) then outputs to a stereo system or a digital recorder.

BIBLIOGRAPHY

Ames, Charles. "Automated Composition in Retrospect: 1956–1986." *Leonardo* 20,2 (1987): 169–185.

Barbaud, Pierre. *Initiation à la composition musicale automatique.* Paris: Dunod, 1966.

Baroni, Mario, and Laura Callegari, eds. *Musical Grammars and Computer Analysis: Atti del Convegno (Modena, 4–6 Ottobre 1982).* Florence: L. S. Olschki, 1984.

Bean, C., Jr. "Information Theory Applied to the Analysis of a Particular Formal Process in Tonal Music." Ph. D. diss. University of Illinois, 1961.

Bharucha, Jamshed. "Music Cognition and Perceptual Facilitation: A Connectionist Framework." *Music Perception* 5,1 (Fall 1987): 1–30.

Bharucha, Jamshed, and Peter Todd. "Modeling the Perception of Tonal Structure with Neural Nets." *Computer Music Journal* 13,4 (Winter 1989): 44–53.

Bolognesi, Tommaso. "Automatic Composition: Experiments with Self-Similar Music." *Computer Music Journal* 7,1 (Spring 1983): 25–36.

Bonanni, Filippo. *Gabinetto armonico pieno d'istromenti sonori indicati e spiegati.* Rome: G. Placho, 1722. Reprinted in 1964 as *The Showcase of Musical Instruments.* New York: Dover Reprints.

Bowles, Edmund. "Musicke's Handmaiden: Or Technology in the Service of the Arts." In *The Computer and Music,* H. Lincoln., ed. Ithaca, N.Y.: Cornell University Press, 1970.

Broeckx, Jan L., and Walter G. Landrieu. "Comparative Computer Study of Style, Based on Five Liedmelodies." *Interface* 1 (April 1972): 29–92.

Brook, Barry S. "Style and Content Analysis in Music: The Simplified 'Plaine and Easie Code'." In *The Analysis of Communication Content,* George Gerbner et al., eds. New York: Wiley, 1969.

Buchner, Alexander. *Mechanical Musical Instruments.* London: Bastchworth Press, 1959.

Cage, John. "HPSCHD." *Source: Music of the Avant Garde* 1 (July 1968): 10–19.

Chomsky, Noam. *Aspects of the Theory of Syntax*. Cambridge, Mass.: MIT Press, 1965.

Cope, David. "Experiments in Music Intelligence." In *Proceedings of the International Computer Music Conference*, San Francisco: Computer Music Association, 1987a.

——— "An Expert System for Computer-Assisted Music Composition." *Computer Music Journal* 11,4 (Winter 1987b): 30–46.

——— "Music and LISP." *AI Expert* 3,3 (March 1988a): 26–34.

——— "Music: The Universal Language." In *Proceedings of the American Association of Artificial Intelligence Workshop on Music and AI*. Menlo Park, Calif.: AAAI, 1988b.

——— "Experiments in Musical Intelligence (EMI): Non-Linear Linguistic-Based Composition." *Interface* 18,1–2 (1989a): 117–139.

——— *New Directions in Music*. 5th ed. Dubuque, Iowa: Wm C. Brown, Co., 1989b.

——— "Pattern Matching as an Engine for the Computer Simulation of Musical Style." In *Proceedings of the 1990 International Computer Music Conference*. San Francisco: Computer Music Association, 1990.

——— "On Algorithmic Representation of Musical Style." In *Musical Intelligence*, M. Balaban, K. Ebcioğlu, and O. Laske, eds. Menlo Park, Calif.: AAAI Press, 1991a.

——— "A Computer Model of Music Composition." In *Machine Models of Music*, Stephan Schwanauer and David Levitt, eds. Cambridge, Mass.: MIT Press, 1991b.

Dodge, Charles, and Curtis Bahn. "Musical Fractals." *BYTE Magazine* 11,6 (June 1986): 185–196.

Dolson, Mark. "Machine Tongues XII: Neural Networks." *Computer Music Journal* 13,4 (Fall 1989): 28–40.

Ebcioğlu, Kemal. *Report on the CHORAL Project: An Expert System for Harmonizing Four-Part Chorales*. Yorktown Heights, N.Y.: IBM Thomas J. Watson Research Center, 1987.

Edgerly, Beatrice. *From the Hunter's Bow*. New York: G. P. Putnam's Sons, 1942.

Forte, A. "Computer-Implemented Analysis of Musical Structure." In *Papers from the West Virginia University Conference on Computer Applications in Music*, Gerald Lefkoff, ed. Morgantown: West Virginia University Library, 1967.

Fucks, W. "Musical Analysis by Mathematics; Random Sequences; Music and Accident." *Gravesaner Blätter* 6,23/4 (1962): 146–170.

Gabura, A. James. "Computer Analysis of Musical Style." In *ACM Proceedings of the 20th National Conference*. New York: Association for Computing Machinery, 1965.

Gjerdingen, Robert. "Using Connectionist Models to Explore Complex Musical Patterns." *Computer Music Journal* 13,3 (Fall 1989): 67–75.

Hiller, Lejaren. "Music Composed with Computers: A Historical Survey." In *The Computer and Music*, H. Lincoln, ed. Ithaca, N.Y.: Cornell University Press, 1970.

Hiller, Lejaren, and Leonard Isaacson. *Experimental Music*. New York: McGraw-Hill, 1959.

Holmes, Thomas. *Electronic and Experimental Music*. New York: Scribner's, 1985.

Holtzman, S. R. "Using Generative Grammars for Music Composition." *Computer Music Journal* 5,1 (Spring 1981): 51–64.

Kastner, Georges. *La harpe d'éole et la musique cosmique*. Paris: G. Brandus, Dufour et Cie, 1856.

Kepler, Johannes. *Harmonices mundi libri V*. Linz, Austria: Johannis Plancus, 1619.

Kircher, Athanasius. *Ars magna lucis et umbrae*. Rome: Ludovici Grignani, 1646.

Kirschen, Yaakov. Music Creator. Ver. 1.0. Walnut, Calif.: JFY, Inc., 1989.

LaRue, Jan. "Two Problems in Music Analysis: The Computer Lends a Hand." In *Computers in Humanistic Research: Readings and Perspectives*, E. A. Bowles, ed. Englewood Cliffs, N.J.: Prentice-Hall, 1967.

Laske, Otto. "In Search of a Generative Grammar for Music." *Perspectives of New Music* 12,1 (Fall-Winter 1973): 351–378.

Lefkoff, Gerald. "Computers and the Study of Musical Style." In *Papers from the West Virginia University Conference on Computer Applications in Music*, Gerald Lefkoff, ed. Morgantown: West Virginia University Library, 1967.

Leman, Marc. "Symbolic and Subsymbolic Information Processing in Models of Musical Communication and Cognition." *Interface* 18,1 and 2 (1989): 141–160.

Lerdahl, Fred, and Ray Jackendoff. *A Generative Theory of Tonal Music*. Cambridge, Mass: MIT Press, 1983.

Levitt, David. "Machine Tongues X: Constraint Languages." *Computer Music Journal* 8,1 (Spring 1984): 9–21.

Lidov, David, and A. James Gabura. "A Melody Writing Algorithm Using a Formal Language Model." *Computer Studies in the Humanities and Verbal Behavior* 4 (1973): 138–148.

Lieberman, Fredric. "Computer-Aided Analysis of Javanese Music." In *The Computer and Music*, H. Lincoln, ed. Ithaca, N.Y.: Cornell University Press, 1970.

Lincoln, Harry, ed. *The Computer and Music*. Ithaca, N.Y.: Cornell University Press, 1970.

Lockwood, Lewis. "Computer Assistance in the Investigation of Accidentals in Renaissance Music." *Report of the Tenth Congress of the International Musicological Society, Ljubljana, 1967*. Kassel: Bärenreiter, 1970.

Loy, Gareth. "Composing with Computers: A Survey of Some Compositional Formalisms and Music Programming Languages." In *Current Directions in Computer Music Research*, Max Mathews and John R. Pierce, eds., Cambridge, Mass.: MIT Press, 1989.

Marcuse, Sibyl. *A Survey of Musical Instruments*. New York: Harper and Row, 1975.

Mathews, Max, and F. R. Moore. "GROOVE: A Program to Compose, Store, and Edit Functions of Time." *Communications of the ACM* 13,12 (December 1970): 715–721.

McPhee, Colin. *Music in Bali*. New Haven: Yale University Press, 1966.

Meier, John. Mozart. Ver. 1.0. Santa Barbara, Calif.: Kinko's Academic Courseware Exchange, 1984.

Mozart, Wolfgang Amadeus. *Musikalisches Würfelspiel*. Mainz: B. Schott's Söhne, Edition 4474.

Murchie, Guy. *Music of the Spheres*. Boston: Houghton Mifflin Company, 1961.

Myhill, John. "Some Simplifications and Improvements in the Stochastic Music Language." In *Proceedings of the 1978 International Computer Music Conference*, Curtis Roads, comp. Evanston, Ill.: Northwestern University Press, 1979.

Nattiez, J.-J. *Fondemonts d'une sémiologie de la musique*. Paris: Union Generale d'Editions, 1975.

Porta, Giovanni Battista. *Magiae naturalis*. Naples, Italy: M. Cancer, 1558.

Ratner, Leonard G. "Ars Combinatoria: Choice and Chance in Eighteenth-Century Music." In *Studies in Eighteenth-Century Music: A Tribute to Karl Geiringer on His Seventieth Birthday*, H. C. Robbins Landon and Roger Chapman, eds. New York: Oxford University Press, 1970.

—— *Classic Music: Expression, Form, and Style*. New York: Schirmer Books, 1980.

Roads, Curtis. "Grammars as Representations for Music." In *Foundations of Computer Music*, Curtis Roads and John Strawn, eds. Cambridge, Mass.: MIT Press, 1985a (an expanded version of the article found in *Computer Music Journal* 3,1 [1979]: 48–55).

—— "An Overview of Music Representations." In *Musical Grammars and Computer Analysis*, M. Baroni and L. Callegari, eds. Florence: Olschki, 1984.

——"Interview with Gottfried Michael Koenig." In *Foundations of Computer Music*, Curtis Roads and John Strawn, eds. Cambridge, Mass.: MIT Press, 1985b.

——"Symposium on Computer Music Composition." *Computer Music Journal* 10,1 (Spring 1986): 40–63.

Ruwet, Nicholas. "Théorie et méthodes dans les études musicales." *Musique en jeu* 17 (1975): 11–36.

Scarborough, Don, Ben Miller, and Jacqueline Jones. "Connectionist Models for Tonal Analysis." *Computer Music Journal* 13,3 (Fall 1989): 49–55.

Schafer, R. Murray. *The Vancouver Soundscape*. Vancouver, Canada: Ensemble Productions (sound recording), 1973.

Schenker, Heinrich. *Five Analyses in Sketchform*. New York: David Mannes School of Music, 1933.

Schillinger, Joseph. *The Mathematical Basis of the Arts*. New York: The Philosophical Library, 1948.

—— *The Schillinger System of Musical Composition*. New York: Da Capo Press, 1978.

Schottstaedt, William. "Automatic Counterpoint." In *Current Directions in Computer Music Research*, Max Mathews and John R. Pierce, eds. Cambridge, Mass.: MIT Press, 1989.

Smoliar, Stephen W. "A Computer Aid for Schenkerian Analysis." *Computer Music Journal* 4,2 (Summer 1980): 41–59.

Spiegel, Laurie. "Sonic Set Theory: A Tonal Music Theory for Computers." In *Proceedings, 2nd Symposium on Small Computers in the Arts, October 15–17, 1982, Philadelphia, Pa.* Los Angeles: IEEE Computer Society, 1982.

Todd, Peter. "A Sequential Network Design for Musical Applications." *Proceedings of the 1988 Connectionist Models Summer School.* San Mateo, Calif.: Morgan Kaufmann, Publishers, 1988.

—— "A Connectionist Approach to Algorithmic Composition." *Computer Music Journal* 13,4 (Winter 1989): 27–43.

Truax, Barry. "The POD System of Interactive Composition Programs." *Computer Music Journal* 1,3 (June 1977): 30–39.

Xenakis, Iannis. *Formalized Music*. Bloomington: Indiana University Press, 1971.

—— "Music Composition Treks." In *Composers and the Computer*, Curtis Roads, ed. Vol. 2, The Computer Music and Digital Audio Series. Madison, Wisc.: A-R Editions, Inc., 1985. (Originally published by William Kaufmann, Inc.)

MUSICAL STYLE REPRESENTATIONS

. . . .

MUSICAL STYLE

Empirical definitions of style seem not to exist. Dickinson (1965) is a massive attempt to refine the basic definition of musical style. Unfortunately, his definition is so vague as to be useless: "Style is the reflection of the individual essence of a work of art which gives it its identity. This identity is the result of a distinctive conjunction of components, coupled with distinctive emphasis among the components" (p. 3). Another recent definition provides narrower guidelines but still does not help us much: "Style is a replication or patterning, whether in human behavior or in the artifacts produced by human behavior, that results from a series of choices made within some set of constraints" (Meyer 1989, p. 3).

Composer Arnold Schoenberg is dubious about the possibilities of defining style. "Since changes of style in the arts do not always mean development, it might be extremely difficult to establish criteria which remain valid in every period of art. But the futility of evaluation deriving from external criteria remains evident throughout the centuries" (Schoenberg 1975, p. 183). Barry Brook comments that "style analysis is in its infancy in the field of musicology. We have much to learn from the techniques and procedures developed in other disciplines and perhaps, especially because of music's abstract nature, something unique to offer in return" (Brook 1969, p. 296).

Apparently, the diversity of styles and definitions of style across the whole of music history make the concept too broad to codify. However, the problem a programmer faces is that a concise and lucid definition is required to program a computer to replicate musical styles. It must transcend the multiple views provided by various historical contexts, perspectives, and resources (Pelinski 1986). Style must be quantifiable or it cannot be transcribed to code.

Classical music analysis provides a static model of structure, but functional representations of chords and melodic indications of motive reticulation (commonplace approaches to analysis in many universities) give little insight into musical *style*. Schenkerian layer techniques, while demonstrating hierarchical structure, obliterate many of the stylistically meaningful attributes of music by stripping away surface material, much of which is critical to evaluation of style (Schenker 1933; Pancharoen 1985).

Of the few rigorous attempts dedicated to delving into the question of style, the work of Guido Adler (1911), Jan LaRue (1967; 1970; 1981), and Leonard Meyer (1989) stands out. LaRue's *Guidelines for Style Analysis* outlines the SHMRG approach, which is based on sound, harmony, melody, and rhythm (as contributing elements) and growth (as a combining element). LaRue also outlines a parallel between language and music based on the model of "syntax-grammar-words" as logical metaphors for "tonality-progressions-chords" (LaRue 1981).

LaRue also considers style analysis as a process originating from the macro-perspective: "The approach to a piece may be likened to the approach of a figure from a distance. Inside a distant blur we first distinguish a head and other parts of the body; then we see eyes in the head; and only at close quarters can we observe the color of the eyes. Similarly for style analysis, the general shape of the piece comes first: we must recognize articulations that define the parts, large and small, before we can trace the progress of ideas and the sources of movement" (LaRue 1970, p. 224). In the work presented later in this volume, I will argue that the converse is the case: The large and small parts must be identified and assembled before the progress of the work can be identified.

Many analysts seek alternative methods. Linguistic parallels, such as studies in context-free grammar, have provoked serious attempts to relate music to language. If these prove viable, they could profoundly alter the theoretical framework of the last century's analytical practices (see Laske 1975; Lidov and Gabura 1973; Winograd 1968). Composers, including myself, have also sought to develop artificially intelligent processes that could not function without high-speed computational power. The combination (unavailable until recently) of digital technologies with linguistic theory holds significant potential for understanding musical style and creating music.

Interestingly, one of the most eloquent proponents of linguistic analysis of music and musical style was Leonard Bernstein (1976). In a series of six lectures given at Harvard (Norton Lectures of 1973), he pointed out that

> in fact, it has been authoritatively suggested that the main reason a serious theory of musical syntax has been so slow to develop is the refusal of music theorists to recognize repetition as the key factor. I think it was Nicholas Ruwet [see discussion in Chapter 1], a distinguished musicologist as well as linguist, who proposed this suggestion. And his argument grows out of a proposition by Roman Jakobson, the great linguistic thinker and one of Chomsky's most influential teachers. Jakobson, speaking of poetry, said (and I reduce this quote): "It is only . . . by the regular reiteration of equivalent units that poetry provides an experience of time . . . comparable to that of musical time." Now that would seem a gross oversimplification, especially if he is referring to the regular reiteration of metrical units. Da-dá, da-dá, da-dá, da-dá hardly produces poetry; it's more like doggerel. But the moment we apply to that mechanical regularity the processes of transformation and variation, we immediately see what he's getting at. (Bernstein 1976, p. 147)

Bernstein's lectures, while deficient in documentation, are amazingly insightful (and influential, as they were widely heard on records and seen on television and on video tape).

Following linguistic procedures as one alternative to traditional models leads one to concepts of musical "verbs," "nouns," and other lexical components. Resolution of a dominant seventh to tonic, for example, may be analogized as a simple "verb-object" motion, the object coming as a consequence of the verb's action, like the tonic coming as a consequence of the dominant motion. This linguistic analogy represents information intuitively available to audiences and metaphorically documents their experience. It is not that musical notes have exact definitions as do words but that they have grammatical counterparts. Rhythm, timbre, articulation, dynamics, envelope, and other musical components also have linguistic parallels.

Knopoff and Hutchinson (1983; 1987) have worked extensively on statistically dissecting the various parameters of musical style, particularly pitch frequencies. They then break the pitch counts into probability curves for the works of certain tonal composers. Their definition, in contrast to that of Dickinson given earlier, emphasizes the statistical analysis of broader characteristics rather than the relative weights of individual elements.

The perspective of the interpreter can sometimes obscure the study of style.

> It is no exaggeration to say that many of the current methods of studying musical style reveal as much about their authors as about the music being examined. . . . We know a good deal about Riemann's attitudes, or Gombosi's, or Schenker's, but really very little about those of Beethoven, Obrecht, or Tchaikowsky. To one degree or another, each of these scholars—and their names are only representative—has allowed a personal belief to color his interpretations, often to the point of obscuring the innate intentions of the composers. (Salop 1971, pp. 17–18)

The work presented later in this volume attempts to avoid the problem of personal bias of the interpreter by building up the analysis of style directly from the works. For any work that can be represented as pitches and durations, the style of the work, to the extent that it is codified in pitches and durations, can be replicated.

Book-length treatises and broad definitions of musical style do not, however, help much in creating computer programs for the replication of musical styles. Having reviewed all of this conjecture, it is clear that some form of definition must be rendered before progressing to a codification of it in the form of computer code. For the purposes of this book, then, "musical style" will mean: *the identifiable characteristics of a composer's music which are recognizably similar from one work to another*. These include, but are not limited to, pitch and duration (the principal elements discussed in this book), timbre, dynamics, and nuance. As well, these elements together constitute grammars perceived on many levels, for instance, as melody, harmony, and counterpoint, which themselves join into introductions, motives, transitions, modulations, and cadences. Combinations of these elements constitute style when they appear repeatedly in two or more works.

TONALITY AND HARMONIC FUNCTION

Vincent D'Indy (Apel 1962, p. 752) described tonality as "the ensemble of musical phenomena which human understanding is able to appreciate by direct comparison with a constant element—the tonic." This focuses on two important elements of tonality. First, it refers to the "ensemble" of musical pitches and chords that typically relate in terms of major and minor keys. Second, it alludes to the functions that these "phenomena" have in relation to the key name pitch and chord (called "tonic"

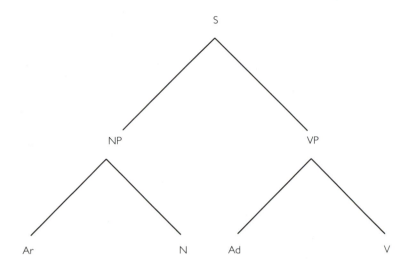

FIGURE 2.1   A diagrammatic representation of the parsing of a sentence into its constituent language parts.

by theorists). Hence, in C major we have an ensemble of notes (C–D–E–F–G–A–B–[C]), which is major, and we have the tonic base—the tonic note C and the tonic chord (triad) C–E–G—to which all the notes relate.

Parsing

Parsing, a technique used in language study, is quite helpful in demonstrating function in music. In language study parsing provides diagrammatic description of the relationship between sentence parts. Figure 2.1 gives a straightforward example of this with a sentence (S) broken into two basic parts—a noun phrase (NP) and a verb phrase (VP). The noun phrase is further broken into an article (Ar) plus a noun (N), and the verb phrase is broken into an adverb (Ad) plus a verb (V).

Compared with the ensemble of notes listed above, parsing a scale provides a more intricate suggestion of the interplay between various components. Figure 2.2 gives one possible way to analyze the notes of a C-major scale. In this diagram, the direction and order of branching has symbolic meaning. Vertical lines show principal functions. Therefore, the C–F–G in the middle row of the chart are the more important pitches of the scale. As well, the location at which an angled line joins a vertical line indicates whether the pitch has ancillary function (higher) or prolongs the main function (lower). Hence, in this analysis, A (which often substitutes for "tonic" C in deceptive cadences) is an ancillary function to C, while E extends the tonic function. Finally the direction of the principal line (the

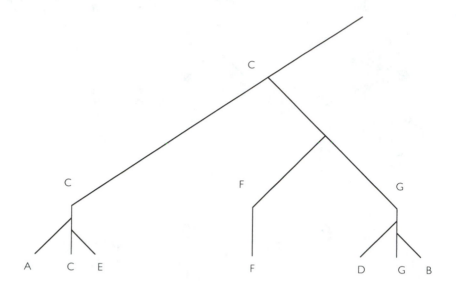

FIGURE 2.2   A parse of the C-major scale.

longest) points at the phrase designation (here, C, the name of the scale). Thus, what appears as a simple parsing is actually a complex differentiation of subtle relationships and subrelationships.

Tonal Functions

In order to lay the groundwork for later chapters, it is necessary to examine a musical example in some detail at this juncture. Those readers who are familiar with music theory may find this material easy going.

Ultimately the tonic (C in the key of C major), dominant (G in the key of C major), and subdominant (F in the key of C major) are the principal actors in tonal music. Other notes either in the key (diatonic) or out (chromatic) all tend to belong to one of those major centers (see Figure 2.2) and can be described as either resolving toward or extending them. Hence the phrase C–D–C–B–G–C in the key of C major could be described as simply tonic to dominant twice with a resolution to tonic at the end. Knowing that notes of a key represent phenomena beyond iteration and gravitate naturally to other notes is critically important to the understanding of tonality.

The top line in Figure 2.3 aptly demonstrates these attributes. All of the notes of a D-major scale (D–E–F♯–G–A–B–C♯–[D]) are presented at one time or another, with D taking a lead role as the first principal downbeat

FIGURE 2.3 Bars 13-17 of Mozart's Piano Sonata No. 6, K. 284, final movement.

and the last note of the phrase. Singing or playing the phrase proves the strength and solidity of D as the tonic of the phrase, a role to which all other notes relate in various ways. Some of the notes, such as scale passages, seem to extend ideas, while others (e.g., the upbeat As and the E before the final tonic) appear to anticipate or prepare pitches that then arrive.

Some refer to this process as "expectation and fulfillment." Tonality allows composers to utilize these known structures for desired results. Mozart embraces tonal resources here, providing the tonic when expected and using other functions (to be described in more detail later) as preparations and extensions of the principal tonic. These tonal techniques are not Mozart's alone but belong to the immense reservoir available to most tonal composers throughout history.

When we consider the full texture in Figure 2.3, the added harmonic component fleshes out the chordal implications of the theme. The rolling Alberti bass outlines chords in typical early Classical style. The D–F♯–A of both the first and last chords solidifies the **D-major context** already implied by the key signature and the melodic line alone. **Blocking the chords,** as in the bottom half of Figure 2.4, helps to clarify their identity. **The resulting** abstracted harmonic progression could have been used by virtually thousands of composers. It is common for keys and key functions to have standard progressions.

One of the most important aspects of tonal music is that chords and pitches have different weights and relationships. As mentioned, these are typically defined as *functions*. Knowing only how to read music and hear individual notes and chords without their inherent function is a bit like knowing about the earth and sun but not their critical orbital relationships. Missing is the knowledge of how eclipses occur and the consequent appreciation and predictability thereof. In music, function incorporates the same kind of pivotal notion of gravity and positioning so important to evaluating structure.

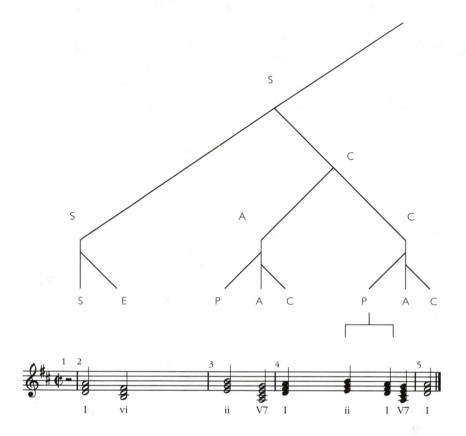

FIGURE 2.4 A harmonic parsing of the theme in Figure 2.3.

The SPEAC System

The SPEAC system, which I developed in 1985 (Cope 1987), is based on ideas, derived from Schenker, that will be discussed in more detail below. It provides another level of abstraction for describing the logical motions of musical notes, harmonies, and motives (groups of notes and harmonies). SPEAC is an acronym with each element described as follows.

The first and most obvious structural role that a chord or melodic idea can represent is *statement*. Notes simply exist "as is" with nothing expected beyond iteration. For the purposes of this book, statements will be identified by the symbol S. Statements don't exist as a result of other activity. They also typically occur near the beginning of musical passages rather than the middle or end. The first chord in Figure 2.4 represents a good example of S.

Statements can be prefaced or lengthened, here called *preparation* (P) and *extension* (E), respectively, or both. Preparations modify the meanings of statements or other identifiers by standing ahead of them without being independent. Extensions may follow any identifier other than another extension or a preparation. In Figure 2.4, measure 3 is a good example of preparation, and the second half of measure 2 is typical of extension. In both cases, the chord sets in each measure have two notes in common. In measure 3, the initial chord prepares the second since the latter is built on the fifth scale degree (A; the relationship between the first and fifth degrees of the scale is more important than other relationships). In measure 2, the second chord extends the more important initial tonic function.

Antecedents (A) cause a significant implication and require resolution. They typically demand a *consequent* (C). Consequents are often the same chords or melodic fragments as found in S. However, they have different implications, the result of a demand for consequence from an antecedent motion. Consider the last two chords of Figure 2.4. This "dominant to tonic" relationship is the strongest in tonal music. So strong is the dominant seventh chord that many find it difficult to hear it performed alone without the subsequent resolution to the tonic function.

Each of these five *identifiers* (SPEAC) relates to one another in prescribed ways. A work cannot begin with a C, for example, since a consequent requires a defined antecedent prior to its occurrence. Likewise, P, by definition, can't end a work. There are many such restrictions. Herein lies an important concept that will play an important role later in this book. *Constraints are better presented as lists of desired results rather than as lists of rules of what should not take place.* In most situations, the number of undesirable procedures far outnumbers the desired. Expressing the latter almost always guarantees more elegant results.

All of this parsing has language equivalents. "I am going to the store!" for example, could easily be represented as S A P C. "I" is a statement. The phrase "am going" sets up a query about where and represents an antecedent requiring (or at least permitting) the consequent "store." The preparatory "to the" simply connects the parts of the sentence with the appropriate grammatical niceties. "I go store" or S A C would communicate the information almost as accurately but less elegantly. The word *store* alone is almost sufficient for saying "I am going to the store," proving the C value of this English-language equivalent of musical patterns. As will be seen later on, the method based on ATN (augmented transition networks) to create the surface translation of language from these representations (e.g., "I" instead of "he," "she," "it," "Bill," etc.) can also offer extraordinary benefits to music composition.

For now, a short analysis of a Mozart phrase will suffice. S E P A C P A C, the parsing shown in Figure 2.4, describes the Mozart phrase shown in Figure 2.3. The preparations (P) and antecedents (A) are in the proper ordering with the consequents (C) a result of the antecedents (A). The extension (E) of the initial statement extends it appropriately. One can also see a hierarchy evolving from this ordering. Since preparations and extensions embellish, they can be defined as less critical to the real structure of the phrase. Hence, as will be discussed later in the chapter, parsing can be a useful tool for the further abstraction of the structural role of the phrase itself.

The function of a C–E–G chord changes depending on key. In C major this chord is tonic, while in F major it is dominant. This is similar to language, in which words can have more than one definition. Also, a C–E–G chord has different functions even in the same key. For example, as the initiator of a phrase it can be a statement, S, while in a cadence it becomes a consequent, C. This too has language parallels—nouns can be subjects in one location and objects in another. Thus, while functions provide insight into surface detail, the SPEAC system in music analysis shows the deeper meaning of the functions.

In Figure 2.4, the Mozart theme has been analyzed (à la the language model) above the staff, and traditional chord symbols (for music theorists) appear below the staff. At the surface level (the lowest level of the parsing diagram), a statement is initially extended. Then two antecedent–consequent actions are elaborated by preparations. The first of these actions, chords 3 through 5, also represents an antecedent of the final, more cadential progression. That is, the second action is stronger in that it ends the phrase and the cadence chord lasts longer. Hence, on a higher hierarchical level, the theme may be analyzed as S A C, represented by the three main branches of the tree in the middle of the parsing diagram.

Analysis using this kind of process strips away stylistic surface detail while at the same time it demonstrates the basic structure of that detail. Since this phrase exists out of context (i.e., not shown preceding or following another), it could be designated hierarchically as an S phrase. Common terminology for this process delineates foreground, middleground, and background, with the first describing the notes themselves, the second the initial processes of abstraction and separation of more important implications, and the latter referring only to the final level of entire phrases and works.

For those not wishing to depend on generic descriptions of protocol and succession rules of SPEAC, Figure 2.5 describes what can follow what.

CURRENT	CAN BE FOLLOWED BY
S	P, E, A
P	S, A, C
E	S, P, A, C
A	E, C
C	S, P, E, A

FIGURE 2.5   Succession rules of the SPEAC abstractions.

Identifiers that follow themselves simply combine to avoid repetition. Substructures shown in preceding paragraphs follow this protocol exactly.

Hierarchical Analysis

Schenkerian analysis, hierarchical and functional by nature, follows roughly these same principles. Heinrich Schenker (1868–1935) demonstrated that music could be understood on three principal levels: foreground, middleground, and background. His analytical approach involved the revealing of each level as one approached a work's *Ursatz* (kernel or fundamental structure). This included a stripping away of elaborations, modifications, or transformations of the foreground through a unique notation that could demonstrate that non-consecutive elements can resolve or extend foreground elements.

Schenker's theories about tonal music have remained controversial since they became more universally known in the 1950s and 1960s. Theorists argue that the very act of removing surface detail to show middle- and background levels strips away the fabric of the music. This very act, some believe, implies that some parts of the music are more important than others and that, while this may be true, such decisions are aesthetic and personal and not subject to deterministic analysis.

While Schenker's theories (and the relevant controversies) are far too elaborate to present in full here, it is important to articulate their relevance to discussions of computers and musical style. Top-down and bottom-up concepts have a very significant impact in programming. Schenker's theories present a detailed bottom-up approach to musical analysis that parallels significantly, when seen in reverse, top-down programming. In other words, the order in which analysis strips away during its attempt to reveal a work's *Ursatz* can be seen as a retrograde of the order of the composing process.

For the purposes of what I feel is critical to the understanding of Schenker's work in the replication of musical styles, the issue of "importance" must be put to rest. For EMI, the hierarchical approach to analysis and composition in no way reflects on a parameter's importance to a given piece of music. First of all, implying relative importance of various aspects of foreground (actual music) of a work would belie the fact that composers vary in the valuation they themselves give these parameters. More important, however, importance varies completely on one's point of view. If the purpose of analysis is to discover generic voice leading, then trills and arpeggiation are relatively unimportant. If, however, your reason for analysis is to discover variations in articulation in performance practice, then these areas are crucial.

The step-by-step reduction of a Bach chorale from foreground to background is shown in Figure 2.6 and demonstrates the property of *prolongation*. This reduction is based on one done by Felix Salzer (Salzer 1962). Here, embellishing chords and harmonies that tend simply to extend the basic function of a primary chord (I IV V) are systematically removed during the analytical process in order to reveal the basic structure of a progression. In the notational system, a notehead with a stem is more important than one without. Each successive level, surface (top) to background (bottom), strips away material on the basis of (1) its embellishing nature as in the first three beats of measure 1 (a passing dominant), (2) its weak functionality as in the G-major triad in the key of A minor, or (3) its prolonging nature as in the material separating the downbeat of the first and third measures. The concept of destination is extremely important as evidenced by the intact cadence and absence of much of the expository part of the double phrase at the deepest level of analysis.

Computers respond quite effectively using these types of representations, progressions, and hierarchies. Rules about identifier ordering can be efficiently described in code. Using these representations, especially the hierarchical model, can be very useful in composing as well.

Form

One way to describe tonal form parallels that of realism in the visual arts. It would be hard to imagine a painter beginning in the upper left-hand corner of a canvas and working slowly across the painting to the lower right. On the contrary, an artist usually sketches a rough

a.

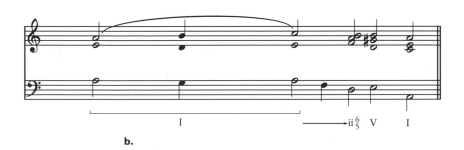

b.

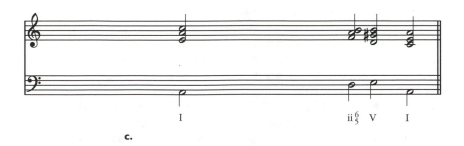

c.

FIGURE 2.6 A Schenkerian analysis of J. S. Bach's Chorale No. 23 based on that of Felix Salzer (1962).

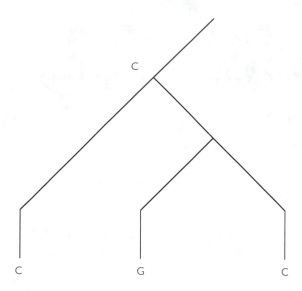

FIGURE 2.7   A parse of a large-scale form. The letters indicate major keys.

charcoal image that describes generally the object to be painted. This is analogous to the assignment of a tonal form before one begins a musical work. At no time does the painter or tonal composer lose sight of the overall thrust or object of the work at hand. Every stroke of the brush, every note from the pen, must fit appropriately into that hierarchically highest conception.

Musical form is then best defined as the highest levels of hierarchy in which a work (or movement) can be described. In tonal music, in which as we have seen function plays a principal role, hierarchy follows the general structure of keys, which are defined by the final cadences of a work's main sections. Parsing according to these concepts reveals a great deal about the larger-scale implications of surface detail. Figure 2.7 demonstrates a three-part structure via previously described means. The note names refer to keys: G major acts as a large-scale extension of or preparation for C major, and the entire structure is said to be in C major. If this structure were used in a standard composition, the material in the first and third sections would likely be much the same, and the G-major section would contrast in some way, though how much and in what ways vary with the composer and the length of the piece. Generally speaking, the shorter the work the more the inner section resembles the initial material. The final cadence of the third section would also likely be more final than that of the first section in order to complete the work rather than just the section. The final cadence of the middle section serves as both the tonic of that section and as the dominant leading to the returning material.

Figure 2.8 follows this structure exactly. The opening theme (first eight bars) holds completely to C major. The second section (beginning bar 9) is in G major (note the F♯s) and contrasts with the opening section by transferring the previous left-hand motion to the right and placing the theme itself in the lower voice. The implied G-major triad at the end of bar 16 serves as a concluding chord to the middle section but moves as well as a dominant back to C major. The final section is exactly like the opening one except for two small but important changes. The A at the end of bar 22 in the right hand and the G on the second beat of the last bar in the left hand are also significant. The A provides just that much more incentive for the last downward movement of the theme toward tonic. The G gives the full dominant-to-tonic cadence that was not found in the use of B on the second beat of bar 8 and thus gives a kind of finality necessary for the end of the work.

Tonal music is fraught with such subtle but critical details. Even though they appear as simple foreground or surface material, they are dictated by the formal structure of the work and only make sense in the discovery of tonal hierarchy present in the form of the work. Figure 2.9 shows the layered complexity of such a structure, beginning with the top level (the statement of the work) down to the surface detail of the first bar of the work.

After the antecedent–consequent qualities of the three major sections are listed, only the structure of the first limb of each tree is explored, simply because of spatial constraints. Nonetheless, the tonal nature of each section and sub-section is apparent. The antecedent–consequent quality of the first two bars (level 2) is topped by the antecedent–consequent quality of the first four bars (level 3), leading in turn to the antecedent–consequent quality of the first eight bars (level 4), and so forth. And, most important, all of this detail can be heard and richly understood by the knowledgeable and experienced tonal listener. Upon analysis, a seemingly simple piano piece can be rendered into a quite complex and deep musical statement. Those aware of the implications of surface details are treated to a special encounter.

Melody

Once one is aware of the hierarchy of embedded structure, the foreground of melody and rhythm can be approached with clarity. These "phenomena," as D'Indy would call them, follow basic tonal principles that generally apply to the combined output of numerous composers over many centuries. They embody: (1) stepwise motion for the most part;

FIGURE 2.8 Schumann's *Trällerliedchen* from his *Album for the Young* (Opus 68), which follows the schematic of Figure 2.7.

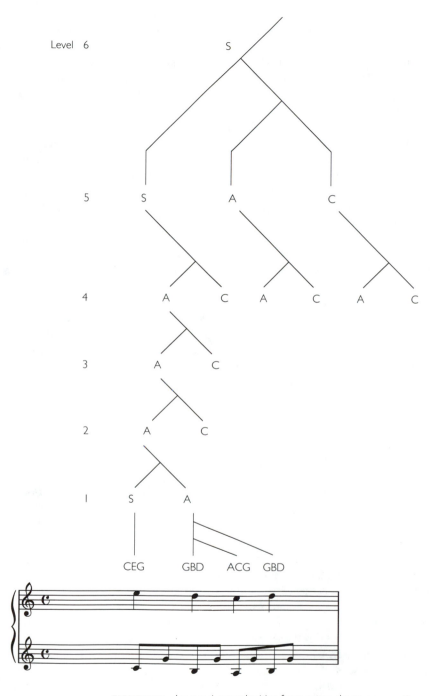

FIGURE 2.9 Layered complexities from a top-down perspective.

(2) compensation of skips by smaller motions in the opposite direction; (3) one or more of the notes per beat agreeing with harmony explicit or implied (typically chords I, IV, or V of the key, due to their harmonic strength). The two melodies examined thus far in the book exemplify these generic rules. Fifty-eight percent of Figure 2.3 and 78 percent of Figure 2.8 are stepwise (or repeated notes), with all but five of the leaps compensated for. Chord tones abound in both figures: Figure 2.3 allows for more non-chord tones due to the fact that it contains more notes per beat in the harmonic rhythm. That is, in Figure 2.3 there are four eighth notes per harmonic rhythmic beat, whereas in Figure 2.8 there are two eighth notes per harmonic rhythmic beat. Figure 2.8 is built almost entirely from chord tones, and the basic harmonic rhythm is assumed to be one chord per quarter note.

Furthermore, tonal melodies usually begin and end on tonic or dominant chord members to ensure proper preparation and cadence. The Mozart melody begins on its lowest note (dominant) and climaxes on its highest (tonic), revolving all the while around the tonic at the beginning of the first measure. The Schumann melody falls within the principal interval of a fifth (C–G), with the opening E as pivot for the passage.

Tonal melodies are often generated, either consciously or subconsciously, from one or more motives (gestures less than a phrase long). These typically fall so naturally into the logic of the line as not to be distinguishable. Motives are varied by transposition (different levels of the scale), by inversion (intervals in the opposite direction), and by extension or truncation.

The motives of the Mozart melody (Figure 2.3) tend to fall into two categories—step (scale) or leap. However, realizing that such a diagnosis could be attributed to any piece in music history suggests care in not abusing the motivic approach to analysis. The scales in the second half of measures 2 and 3, however, are distinctive and rate as variations of one another. The two gestures beginning on beats 1 and 2 in measure 4 likewise deserve mention.

The Schumann melody (Figure 2.8) is so scalar that only direction and rhythm allow the motives to be recognized. Here the first two bars convincingly present an antecedent motive, to which the ensuing two bars, of a skip-step nature, act as consequent. The melodic change in the final bar provides the aforementioned cadential quality necessary to tonally close the passage.

Within all of this discussion of the generic quality of tonal melodies lies the first real insight into the personal and stylistic quality of certain motives. Composers of tonal music often found certain melodic motives of more interest than others and used these extensively in more than one work. Consider the five examples in Figure 2.10. All come at cadence

FIGURE 2.10 Five cadential patterns taken from Mozart piano sonatas. a) No. 6, K. 284 (1775), second movement, m. 91. b) No. 10, K. 330 (1778), second movement, mm. 27–28. c) No. 10, K. 330 (1778), third movement, mm. 15–16. d) No. 16, K. 545 (1788), second movement, mm. 15–16. e) No. 17, K. 547a (1788), first movement, mm. 181–82.

points in major keys. All are by Mozart, though at various times in his career (1775 to 1788). The first two are most similar by virtue of their intervallically identical sixteenth-note introductory patterns. The latter three are variants of one another, each beginning with a minor second and then skipping down a minor triad. Each is in different keys, employs slightly different rhythms, and has varying lengths and textures. And yet the contour, interval content, and placement all contribute to recognition on the listener's part.

Looking back at the first melody example in Figure 2.3 and examining the cadential figure leads one to the realization that in the final notes of a very simple tonal melody lies a characteristic signal of the melody's composer. His signature (see definition below) is neatly hidden in the fabric of routine tonal garb—the last six notes of the melody. The rhythm is varied and the key different (though major), but the recognizable contour nonetheless betrays the unmistakable identity of Mozart.

A *signature* is a set of contiguous intervals (i.e., exempt from key differences) found in more than one work by the same composer. Signatures typically contain two to nine notes melodically and more if combined with harmonies. They are generally divorced from rhythm, though rhythmic ratios often remain intact. Signatures are work-independent. They do not sound as if they come from a certain work of a composer but rather from the style of a composer (or a group of composers). One good example of this would be the Landini cadence, a particularly obvious example from the fourteenth century. This cadence incorporates the melodic movement of the sixth scale degree out to the octave and has such a distinguishing sound as to be unmistakable.

Another example of a signature would be Mozart's (and other composers of his time) use of a lower chromatic pitch resolving upward by a half-step. Figure 2.11 gives four examples of its use. In each case the appoggiatura is chromatic and provides varying degree of dissonance to the harmonic accompaniment. In Figure 2.11a, the F♯ in the final bar, along with its resolution (G), is the non-harmonic tone signature. In Figure 2.11b, the notes C♯, D♯, G♯ and F♯ in successive bars of the example are all versions of the same signature. The downbeats in Figure 2.11c demonstrate a use of the signature as they do in bars 16 and 18 of Figure 2.11d. Mozart's music abounds with rhythmically different versions of this signature, and while other composers may use it, it helps listeners (especially when heard with other signatures) to identify Mozart as the composer of the work.

Leonard Meyer (1989) calls the use of patterns (ubiquitous in a period of musical history or particular to a given style) as *strategic play*. His mention of the terms *stock* and *formula* tend to indicate that for him, at least, what has been called signatures herein is a relatively minor component in the larger definition of musical style itself. He remarks: "Both from the rule-governed melodic, harmonic, and metric relationships and from repeated encounters with this specific figure, the competent listener knows (though perhaps tacitly) this is a pattern that customarily closes a phrase, section, or movement" (p. 26). While the attention Meyer pays this concept is small, the insight is significant, given the lack of attention other sources pay it.

"The organic development of art requires masters who hold the bridle taut in their hands. A truly individual style is found among those pillar figures across music history whose individual personality is strong enough

FIGURE 2.11 From Mozart's a) Piano Concerto No. 21, K. 467 (1785), second movement, mm. 2–4. b) Sonata No. 1, K. 279 (1774), first movement, mm. 5–8. c) Symphony No. 40, K. 550 (1788), second movement, mm. 71–79. d) Sonata No. 8, K. 311 (1777), first movement, mm. 15–18.

FIGURE 2.11   continued.

to express itself inside the very stylistic limits of an artistic genre that they themselves have respected." Thus wrote Guido Alder in 1911 in his much heralded book on musical style. More simply put—personal style, if it is strong enough, rises from a larger set of constraints imposed by the music of the time. Strength is interpreted here to mean "signature."

Texture and Counterpoint   .

As one begins to move away from the generic indicators of tonal music toward those that afford composer choice and hence tend to contribute to style, depth of texture and degree of counterpoint become significant. Even a quick glance through a book of Mozart sonatas, for example, will verify that his textures rarely exceed three simultaneously sounding voices with often only one or two notes sounding at a time. Textures vary from phrase to phrase but rarely within a phrase itself, except at cadence points to enhance the quality or finality of a closure.

On the other hand, Schumann often has six or more voices in texture, with changes occurring rarely except between entire sections. Knowing both the texture of a composer's style as well as the frequency of variation can be an effective aid in discovering style.

The degree of counterpoint present in a style can also indicate its composer. On the one hand, contrapuntal extremes such as formal fugues, chordal works of pure homophony, or both are somewhat rare. On the other hand, the level of imitation of melodic voices found in bass lines can indicate the styles of but a few tonal composers. Mozart, for example, while lean in texture, rarely imitates melodic lines in the bottom line, relegating the bass to various ostinati or traditional early Classical repeating motives. Schumann, however, as seen by his work from *Album for the Young* (Figure 2.8), doubles the melody in the bass line throughout. While this imitation occurs simultaneously with the statement in the upper voice, it does suggest contrapuntal techniques beyond tonal clichés.

Mozart is content to vary inherited ostinati, as seen in the examples in Figure 2.12 from 1774 to 1788. In each case, Mozart has used basically the same motive for his accompaniment. Obviously, since each example comes from a different work, they are not based on any local theme. At the same time, Mozart varies the motive in rhythm, duration, and interval content so that one is subtly surprised by the alterations. This ostinato is used by many other composers including Mozart's early teacher Franz Joseph Haydn. None, however, puts it into so many different guises as does Mozart. It is the art of pushing the ostinato into variation, not its simple presence, that is Mozart's gift and indicator of his style.

In contrast, Schumann's imitative counterpoint abounds throughout his music. In the example in Figure 2.13, the opening motive occurs in successive additions of voices. The imitation is very apparent in the left hand here, even though the rhythm and pitches are not exactly the same as in the melody given in the right hand at the beginning of the example. The last cadence ends with a three-note Classic-Romantic signature in the bass voice. One finds this omnipresent in the music of tonal composers from the early seventeenth to late nineteenth centuries as another device to help ensure that the final cadences present more closure than similar internal ones. The texture and counterpoint of this example contrast with those of Mozart shown previously.

Studying the basic context provided by Classical tonal music and the harmonic and hierarchically formal frames it provides highlights the hidden characteristics of various composers' styles. Melodic signatures, textural differences, and subtle elements of counterpoint all contribute to a differentiation of one composer from another. These revelations also provide clear ways of representing these characteristics in the body of a computer language and a system of computational representations, which are the subject of ensuing chapters.

a.

b.

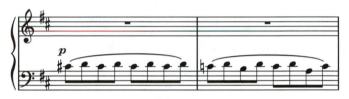

c.

d.

FIGURE 2.12   Variations of a signature from works by Mozart.
a) Piano Sonata No. 5, K. 283 (1774), third movement, m. 123.
b) Piano Sonata No. 6, K. 284 (1775), first movement, m. 88
c) Piano Sonata No. 7, K. 309 (1777), first movement, mm. 33-34.
d) Piano Sonata No. 10, K. 330 (1778), third movement, m. 131.
e) Piano Sonata No. 13, K. 333 (1778), third movement, m. 24.
f) Piano Concerto No. 23, K. 488 (1786), first movement, m. 114.
g) Piano Sonata No. 16, K. 545 (1788), first movement, m. 13.
h) Piano Sonata No. 17, K. 547a (1788), first movement, m. 27.

e.

f.

legato

g.

h.

FIGURE 2.12 continued.

Generating Hierarchies

Composing phrases of language or music is quite differ-ent from analyzing them. Finding form in works of art, be they stories or compositions, is not difficult. The reverse, that of putting it there in the first place, even if one reverses the same analytical process used to decipher a work, is not at all a simple matter. Choosing a proper sequence of nouns,

FIGURE 2.13   From Schumann's *Album for the Young* ("Kleiner Morgenwanderer").

verbs, and other word types and then randomly substituting words of that type generally produces gibberish, as in "noun-verb-noun" and "horse-grabs-sky," for example.

Consider the brief paragraph in Figure 2.14a. These four sentences represent perfectly generated examples of word types. Protocols of what types of words can precede and follow each other (succession rules) have been adhered to exactly. Unfortunately, there is little meaning to any of the generations; there is no flesh, just the skeleton of a language. Machines, however, work very efficiently with this aspect of grammar. If we employ and ascribe rules to only a few word types, programming logical functions that produce absolutely correct sentences from representations (i.e., noun, verb, adverb, etc.) is routine.

For machines to translate such generations into meaningful paragraphs requires less trivial programs. The programmer can make arbitrary initial choices that force more and more constraints into play. Initial choices fall on particularly important word types and not on "adjectives," "prepositions," or "articles." These latter word types are less material to the meaning of the paragraph, and the selections can depend on which "nouns," "verbs,"

Proper-noun-possessive adjective noun adverb verb preposition article noun. Pronoun adjective noun adverb verb preposition article noun. Article adjective noun verb adverb. Proper-noun verb preposition article adjective noun.

a.

Bill's adjective noun adverb verb preposition article noun. Pronoun adjective noun adverb verb preposition article noun. Article adjective noun verb adverb. **Bill** verb preposition article adjective noun.

b.

Bill's adjective **cat** adverb verb preposition article noun. **Her** adjective noun adverb verb preposition article noun. Article adjective noun verb adverb. **Bill** verb preposition article adjective noun.

c.

Bill's adjective **cat** adverb **ran** preposition article noun. **Her** adjective noun adverb **clawed** preposition article noun. Article adjective noun **loosened** adverb. **Bill laughed** preposition article adjective noun.

d.

Bill's adjective **cat furiously ran** preposition article **twine**. **Her** adjective **paw anxiously clawed** preposition article **ball**. Article adjective noun **loosened immediately**. **Bill laughed** preposition article adjective noun.

e.

Bill's feisty cat furiously ran to the twine. Her furry paw anxiously clawed at the ball. The yellow string loosened immediately. Bill laughed at the amusing sight.

f.

FIGURE 2.14 a) An example of proper syntax. b) Arbitrary incipient choice of *Bill* as a major character. c) The addition of *cat* as the second major character. d) The addition of verbs. e) The addition of adverbs. f) A complete translation of the preceding parsed syntax.

and "adverbs" are chosen. The adjectives, prepositions, and articles can be filled in, therefore, when the nouns, verbs, and adverbs have been selected.

For example, the paragraph in Figure 2.14b is exactly like the first, except that the "proper-noun" *Bill* has been chosen randomly as the name

Tonic (noun? solid, fundamental, cadential)
Supertonic (pronoun? predominant)
Mediant (adjective? part of the tonic family)
Subdominant (adverb? predominant)
Dominant (verb? requiring resolution)
Submediant (article? postmediant)
Leading-tone (preposition? pretonic)

FIGURE 2.15   Possible linguistic equivalents of diatonic chord representations.

of a major character of the text. The other proper-noun present in the paragraph immediately reverts to the same name. This process is non-linear: That is, the first *Bill* specified could have been the one in the last sentence, forcing the "possessive" form recursively into the first sentence.

Now the program can choose other important word types. By adding *cat* as the second major character in the paragraph, a gender choice has been made at the beginning of the second sentence (Figure 2.14c). When we add verbs the meaning of the paragraph begins to emerge: "laughed", "ran," and "clawed" surface as extremely important descriptions of action (Figure 2.14d). Adverbs, though less important than verbs, add yet another dimension (Figure 2.14e). The final preposition now has to be *at* because one laughs *at* things. And, while many possibilities exist for the first adjective, the choice has only surface importance. Figure 2.14f shows the final "translation."

Tonal music has developed theoretical representations comparable to those of language. The diatonic chord representations (tonic, supertonic, etc.) are called functions and exist as scale degrees (C, D, etc., in C major) and as chords built on these scale degrees. In tonal music, the order of these notes and especially chords is very important. Succession rules, very similar to the language model, work effectively in generating correct arrangements. Figure 2.15 shows the diatonic chord representations (successive triads completely within the given key, beginning with the first note of the key) and their comparisons to language. While very subjective, these are meant to give the reader some indication of their grammatical parallel. Figure 2.16 shows a full musical paragraph.

Looking at music in this way is not new. A number of theorists (see LaRue 1967; Lerdahl and Jackendoff 1983; Roads 1986; Longuet-Higgins 1987; Longuet-Higgins and Lisle 1989; Baroni 1983) have noted similarities in parsing models and generally applied the principles of grammar to

Tonic mediant subdominant dominant tonic. Supertonic subdominant dominant submediant dominant tonic. Leading tone tonic subdominant supertonic dominant tonic. Mediant submediant subdominant dominant tonic.

FIGURE 2.16 An example of proper musical (tonal) syntax. Periods represent cadence points.

music. Following the same methodology of non-linear and recursive translation leads to the results, parallel to that of language, shown in Figure 2.17a. Again, arbitrary initial choices lead to an ever-increasing level of constraints.

In some ways, by choosing the key of C, almost all of the remaining choices are predefined since each function is tied to a particular scale degree and an associated diatonic triad. Thankfully, inversion (stacking the notes of a chord in a different order) and substitution (adding another pitch such as a seventh) allow a variety of choices for a given representation. Figure 2.17b shows how substitutions provide variety: Different varieties of dominant chords allow for creative manipulation of translation. In the next to the last cadence, the leading tone functions as a dominant. A final run in Figure 2.17c shows the completed musical generation. Note how the full dominant seventh chord has been saved for the penultimate function of the fourth phrase. This exemplifies the effects of the non-linear approach—the final cadence is more substantial because from the outset its importance to the small work was known.

There are further important reasons that this approach becomes critical to machine composition. First, parsing extracts the rules of protocol for chord functions. Generating new musical material from correctly derived parsings guarantees that new compositions will follow the correct successions in the original music. This ensures that the process will not be a simple wandering process of creation often found in "rules only" programs. Second, chord abstractions, as with word representations, are hierarchical. Important functional decisions are made first, with less important choices saved for last. The compositional process moves smoothly from a logical ordering of tonics and dominants to mediants and submediants. Each generation in Figure 2.17 is a further translation of the progression above it. Finally, generating sections from previously generated *movements*, rather than just phrases (musical sentences), allows for formal hierarchy and for chord-to-chord relationships to be composed. A chord inversion, appropriate at the end of a second phrase, for example, would be unacceptable at the end of a section.

(C-E-G) mediant subdominant dominant **(C-E-G)**. Supertonic subdominant dominant submediant dominant **(E-G-C)**. Leading tone **(C-E-G)** subdominant supertonic dominant **(C-E-G)**. Mediant submediant subdominant dominant **(C-E-G)**.

a.

(C-E-G) mediant subdominant **(G-B-D)(C-E-G)**. Supertonic subdominant **(B-D-G)** submediant **(G-B-D)** **(E-G-C)**. Leading tone **(C-E-G)** subdominant supertonic **(B-D-F)** **(C-E-G)**. Mediant submediant subdominant **(G-B-D-F)** **(C-E-G)**.

b.

(C-E-G) (E-G-B) (F-A-C) (G-B-D) (C-E-G). (F-A-C-D) (F-A-C) (B-D-G) (A-C-E) (G-B-D) (E-G-C). (D-B-F) (C-E-G) (A-C-F) (D-F-A-C) (B-D-F) (C-E-G). (E-G-B) (A-C-E) (F-A-C) (G-B-D-F) (C-E-G).

c.

FIGURE 2.17   a) Arbitrary initial choice of C-E-G as a main chord of the syntax. b) Further realization of the syntax. c) A full-scale surface.

Formal development entails correctly generating complete phrases from sections of a work. For example, imagine the progressions shown in Figure 2.18. The first instance represents a work with three major sections that have the properties of the harmonic functions shown. The vertical lines indicate that the representation below is a legal substitution for the single function immediately above. Hence, the second line, "(dominant tonic)," is an expansion of "tonic" in the first line. By virtue of ending with a tonic, this second line is a good generation of a "tonic" substitution. The third line shows a phrase ending with the typical tonal antecedent "dominant," which demonstrates how it correctly substitutes for the "dominant" chord in line two. This is then translated into actual notes.

This process assures that every level of the compositional process results not in wandering chords but in a fleshing out of very important functional relationships. Hence, every level verifies every other level by validating elements of macro cadences and implicit antecedent–consequent motion. This reverse Schenker approach (i.e., compositional rather than analytical) seems especially natural, musical, and logical. Computational composition seems particularly well suited to the inherent logic of this approach.

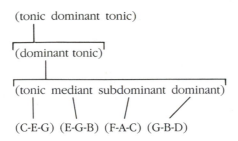

FIGURE 2.18 Formal generation of harmonic functions.

Thus, as in the generation of grammatical structures, the machine may start from a simple plot and then, by expanding through correctly implemented generation, can create a full, final translation, every element of which corresponds to the initial inspiration and, while arbitrary, seems dictated or inevitable at the time of performance.

Augmented Transition Networks (ATNs)

Augmented transition networks (ATNs) help vary output and generate extended examples of natural language processing. ATNs were crystallized and popularized by William Woods (1970) of Harvard and were based on previous work by (in particular) Bobrow and Fraser (1969). Since then, the ATN formalism has been widely used (Bolc 1983; McTear 1987) for question-answering systems, speech-processing systems, language-generation systems, modeling learning, and even for processing visual information. It has also become one of the standard tools of computational linguistics (Johnson 1983). ATNs have been used to implement many functioning natural language systems (Pereira and Warren 1980). Referring to the power of ATNs, Christaller and Metzing remark:

> Here was a formalism of the same power as a transformational grammar, as a means of characterising sentence structures and structural relationships, but one whose operational claims could be clearly stated, and which, in addition, provided a "surface grammar," i.e. provided a means of obtaining a sentence surface structure from the given input string. (Christaller and Metzing 1983, p. 44)

A "transition network" consists of interconnecting states that end subphrases of sentences, initiate correct new phrase sub-sections, or do both. Transition networks are initiated at the sentence level, with each sub-level (sub-phrase) structure generated until word representation occurs. The SPEAC system (discussed earlier in this chapter) is one example of a transition network, if one imagines its succession rules as the nodal junctures between sub-phrases and word representations. Augmenting such a network (to achieve ATN) involves recursion through transition networks such that logical variations and extensions of the material can be generated. In the first case (variation), different sentences that say basically the same thing can be produced for variety. In the second case (extensions), sentences initiate the production of paragraphs, paragraphs initiate the production of sections, and so forth.

Stepping though an example should prove helpful. A sentence analyzing algorithm is shown in Figure 2.19 (after McTear 1987). The first (top) level of Figure 2.19 is a left-to-right representation of a sentence composed of two phrases: a noun phrase and a verb phrase. The notations "S_0," "S_1" and "S_{final}" represent nodes that end a preceding action (e.g., "Seek Noun Phrase" preceding "S_1") and initiate a new action (e.g., "Seek Verb Phrase" following "S_1"). The second representation—"Noun Phrase (NP)"—is one possible expansion of the first section of the top sentence. The purpose here is to evolve word representations (e.g., "Article") or further phrases already or yet to be defined. The recursive loop in "NP_1" shows an optional adjective modifying the "Noun" in the "NP" being developed. The "jump" between "NP_2" and "NP_{final}" indicates that the "Prepositional Phrase" may be deleted, the opposite of the recursive adjective just discussed. The third and fourth representations (i.e., "Verb Phrase [VP]" and "Prepositional Phrase [PP]") should be self-explanatory, following these same principles. It should be noted that the definition of the final "Noun Phrase" can be found already described in the representation "NP" two levels above it.

Figure 2.20 shows a simple dictionary that can be used to construct actual sentences, using the approach shown in Figure 2.19. This simple dictionary allows a number of alternative structures to be generated. For example, while a noun phrase must consist of an article and a noun, many can be written: "a man," "the man," and so forth. In addition, according to our definition in Figure 2.19, it may or may not have an adjective or a prepositional phrase (e.g., "the little man" or "the man in the park").

Using the information of Figures 2.19 and 2.20 could produce, for example, the following: "The man saw the little white mouse in the park." New sentences that mean the same thing but say it differently can also be created: "A man saw the little white mouse"; "The man saw a mouse"; "A man saw the little mouse in a park"; "A man saw the white mouse." Each of these variants is achievable through instructions at the nodal points (the circles) in the diagrams of Figure 2.19. These nodal points determine the possible situations in which a subsequent generation can be skipped (i.e., "jump") or elaborated upon (e.g., "adjective").

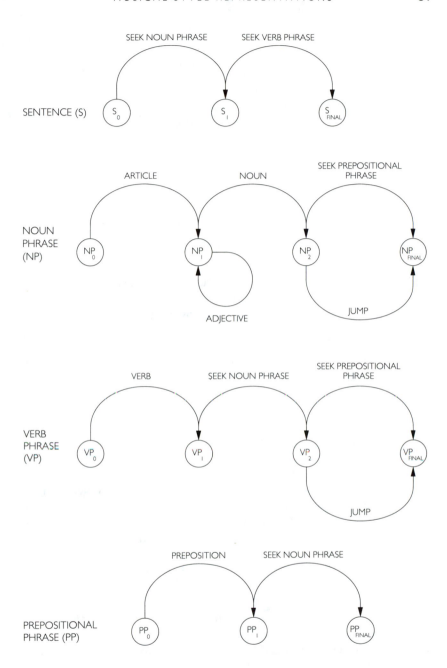

FIGURE 2.19 Phrase structure rules.

Dictionary

the	article (AR)
a	article (AR)
man	Noun (N)
mouse	Noun (N)
park	Noun (N)
little	Adjective (ADJ)
white	Adjective (ADJ)
saw	Verb (V)
in	Preposition (P)

FIGURE 2.20   A simple dictionary based on the grammar of Figure 2.19.

Recursing through the syntax expansions of Figure 2.19 while remembering the current states of the nodes allows for the production of new material as well. For example, "The man saw the little white mouse in the park. The little white mouse saw the man in the park" extends the material in meaningful and useful ways. Obviously, with this tiny dictionary, one is not able to take this example much further. However, using an ATN with more complicated syntax and extended dictionaries can promote the creation of more interesting and developed text.

The diagram in Figure 2.21 is a bit more complicated. It demonstrates how, with very little information, interesting new generations from very little material can take place. The structure operates from left to right, with free choices listed above and below the central nodes. Choices dependent on circumstance are forced when sequences above and below the center line are not joined by a common node. In this case, once a choice has been made, it must be adhered to until another common (to both lower and upper regions) nodal point has been reached. Hence, the choice of "symphony" leads directly to composers of symphonies and the choice of "opera" to composers of operas. The choice of "song" and "aria" also leads to "sing" instead of "play." While in Figure 2.14 the component elements are fixed, in Figure 2.21 these elements may be expanded or contracted by the use of conditional code at each node.

Figure 2.22 shows how similar constructs with musical note patterns can generate legitimate phrase structures in music. Following roughly the same design as the language ATN algorithm, the musical version produces logical phrases (see Figure 2.23) with style relevance (in this case Mozart). The ATN follows metrical constraints ($\frac{4}{4}$ on top, $\frac{3}{4}$ below) as a parallel to the type shown in the previous linguistic generation. Since signatures are of various sizes that are not necessarily convenient for metric placement, the version (top in Figure 2.22) is skewed in that the cadential signatures have three beats. However, the results in the final cadence of Figure 2.23b survive the anomaly, as is typically the case when using signatures. Note that space limitations have prevented the inclusion of the accompaniments to any but the signatures of the examples in Figure 2.22. Interestingly, accompaniments may be separated from their melodic counterparts and stored by function for later use with other melodies requiring accompaniments of the same function. This can provide for further ATN variation.

Obviously, the transitions in Figure 2.23 are rough (although they can be smoothed by a deeper ATN). However, the language metaphor holds, despite the triviality of the results (from both examples of ATN). With proper selection of elemental representations (i.e., nouns = tonics) and careful coding of appropriate local semantics, the same program that produces sentences can produce music. As Curtis Roads points out:

> Augmented Transition Network (ATN) grammars are equivalent in generative power to Chomsky's transformational grammar. In the ATN paradigm, the grammar is represented as a finite-state automaton with recursion. The advantage of ATN grammars is that several types of nodes within the automaton allow very flexible parsing or generating behavior to be implemented.
>
> For example, certain nodes of the automaton may represent conditional tests which must be passed before proceeding on to the next structure-generating node. Other nodes operate on already-generated tree structures. Hence, the ATN formalism allows transformational operations to be embedded in the parse without the need for a separate transformational component. Finally, ATN grammars allow branches to arbitrary . . . code, providing more-or-less unrestricted computational possibilities.
>
> An ATN grammar is not just a conceptual model. . . . Although the ATN model has been widely used in natural language processing, it has not yet been adapted for any musical purpose. (Roads 1986, p. 21)

Arnold Salop, however, points out the dangers of such an approach:

> It is very clear . . . that music consists of something more than a series of isolated evocative effects. Suppose that all of the effects contained in a Beethoven sonata were presented, but in some kind of random order. Let us say that a tape recording of the sonata could be cut into foot-long segments, the segments thrown into the air, and then the whole reassembled in whatever order the segments fell to the ground. Almost certainly such a patchwork opus would lose a great deal of the sense of coherent meaning so obvious in the original version. (Salop 1971, pp. 19–20)

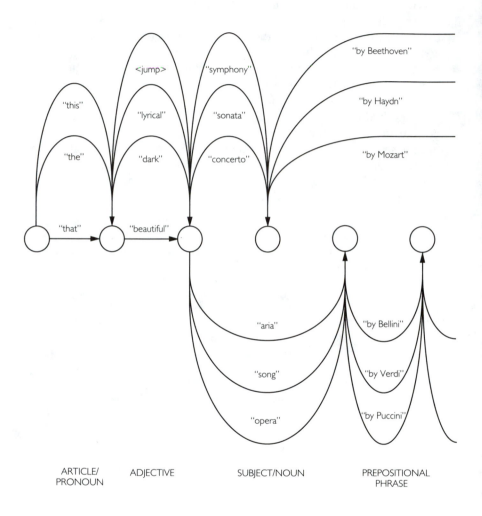

ARTICLE/   ADJECTIVE   SUBJECT/NOUN   PREPOSITIONAL
PRONOUN   PHRASE

FIGURE 2.21   Diagrammatic expression of a language ATN.

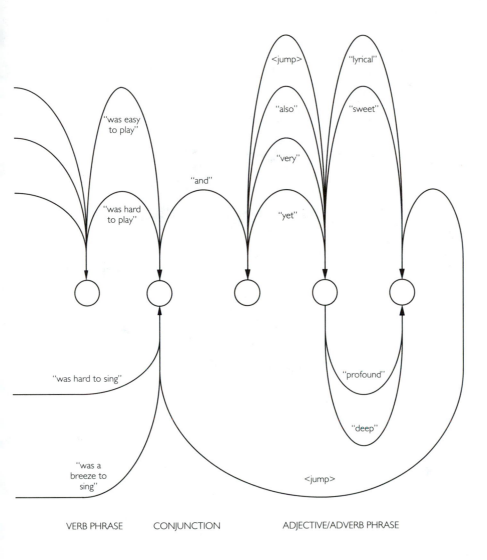

VERB PHRASE   CONJUNCTION   ADJECTIVE/ADVERB PHRASE

FIGURE 2.21   continued.

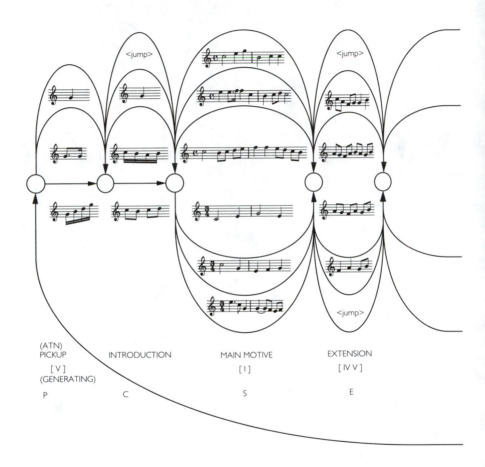

FIGURE 2.22   A simple musical ATN.

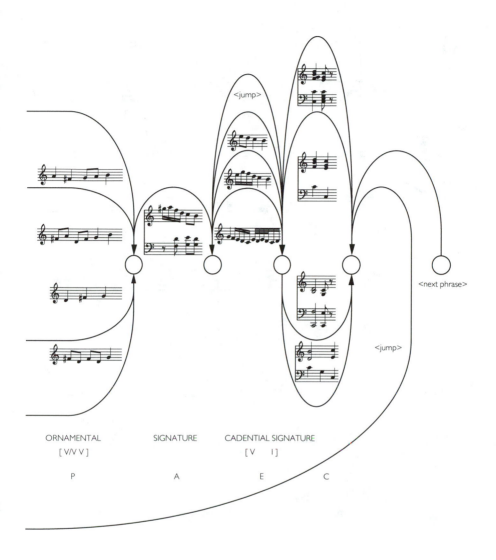

FIGURE 2.22   continued.

FIGURE 2.23   Two possible realizations of Figure 2.22.

Obviously, random splicing of musical segments of a single (or even more than one) work (except those created as Mozart did in his K. Anh. 294d specifically to make correct realizations inevitable) would produce gibberish. However, intricate analysis of music for the application of a hierarchical ATN allows for the discovery of applicable nodal points and enhances the ability of computational systems to create new works in given styles. Such analysis would include key and metric sensitivity, chord function interchanges, pattern matching, and use of the SPEAC system discussed in this chapter (note the analysis at the bottom of Figure 2.22). And, unlike Mozart's *Musikalisches Würfelspiel*, these are location-sensitive combinations. All of these ensure that recombinant gestures do not become, in Salop's phrase, a "patchwork opus."

It is clear that ATN creates a powerful tool for generating varying combinations of proper sentences, provided that lexicons as to what constitutes appropriate nouns, noun phrases, and so on are given. Imagine, however, that such lexicons must be derived from analysis of already extant literature in order to extract style as well as merely allowable combinations. Not only would such a lexicon have to define each word as constituent "noun," and so forth, but it must also relate it to the appropriate place in the order of the sentence (i.e., "subject," "object"). This creates complexities an order of magnitude larger than simply recombining verbal text. Yet this is the problem facing programmers when ATN is applied through automated music systems. The SPEAC system combined with pattern matching offers solutions to this problem by cataloging musical elements and groups of elements into lexicons or dictionaries.

As with the linguistic ATN, the success or failure of efforts to generate grammatically correct music depends on these appropriately constructed dictionaries of harmonies (notes–word equivalents) and motives (signatures–phrase equivalents). As previously stated, these are stored in EMI according to the SPEAC system of identifiers. This ensures that the results are non-chaotic. Using function equivalents similar to Chomsky's (1965) transformational grammar, entrances and exits to these ATN matches are made logical and made to conform to the musical parsings of the original style in the database.

Chapter 3 will provide a LISP program based on the language aspect of this chapter, and Chapter 4 will show how to build programs that realize the musical ATN introduced here.

BIBLIOGRAPHY

Adler, Guido. *Der Stil in der Musik*. Leipzig: Breitkopf and Härtel, 1911.

Apel, Willi. *Harvard Dictionary of Music*. Cambridge, Mass.: Harvard University Press, 1962.

Baroni, Mario. "The Concept of Musical Grammar." *Music Analysis* 2,2 (1983): 175–208.

Bernstein, Leonard. *The Unanswered Question: Six Talks at Harvard.* Cambridge, Mass.: Harvard University Press, 1976.

Bobrow, D. G., and J. B. Fraser. "An Augmented State Transition Network Analysis Procedure." In *Proceedings of the International Joint Conference on Artificial Intelligence,* Donald Walker and Lewis M. Norton, eds. San Mateo, Calif.: Morgan Kaufmann, 1969.

Bolc, Leonard. *The Design of Interpreters, Compilers, and Editors for Augmented Transition Networks.* Berlin: Springer-Verlag, 1983.

Brook, Barry S. "Style and Content Analysis in Music: The Simplified 'Plaine and Easie Code'." In *The Analysis of Communication Content,* George Gerbner et al., eds. New York: Wiley, 1969.

Chomsky, Noam. *Aspects of the Theory of Syntax.* Cambridge, Mass.: MIT Press, 1965.

Christaller, Thomas, and Dieter Metzing. "Parsing Interactions and a Multi-Level Parser Formalism Based on Cascaded ATNs." In *Automatic Natural Language Parsing,* Sparck Jones and Y. Wilks, eds. Chichester, England: Ellis Horwood Limited, 1983.

Cope, David. "Experiments in Music Intelligence." In *Proceedings of the International Computer Music Conference,* San Francisco: Computer Music Association, 1987.

Dickinson, Sherman. *A Handbook of Style in Music.* Poughkeepsie, N.Y.: Vassar College, 1965.

Johnson, R. "Parsing with Transition Networks." In *Parsing Natural Language,* Margaret King, ed. New York: Academic Press, 1983.

Knopoff, Leon, and William Hutchinson. "Entropy as a Measure of Style: The Influence of Sample Length." *Journal of Music Theory* 27,1 (Spring 1983): 75–97.

—— "The Clustering of Temporal Elements in Melody." *Music Perception* 4,3 (Spring 1987): 281–303.

LaRue, Jan. "Two Problems in Music Analysis: The Computer Lends a Hand." In *Computers in Humanistic Research: Readings and Perspectives,* E. A. Bowles, ed. Englewood Cliffs, N.J.: Prentice-Hall, 1967.

—— *Guidelines for Style Analysis.* New York: W. W. Norton and Co., 1970.

——— "The Quadrant Framework for Style Analysis in Music." *Journal of the College Music Society* 21,1 (Spring 1981): 40–47.

Laske, O. "Musical Semantics: A Procedural Point of View." *Proceedings of the 1st International Congress on the Semiotics of Music, Belgrade, 17–21 Oct. 1973.* Pesaro: Centro di Iniziativa Culturale, 1975.

Lerdahl, Fred, and Ray Jackendoff. *A Generative Theory of Tonal Music.* Cambridge, Mass.: MIT Press, 1983.

Lidov, David, and A. James Gabura. "A Melody Writing Algorithm Using a Formal Language Model." *Computer Studies in the Humanities and Verbal Behavior* 4 (1973): 138–148.

Longuet-Higgins, Christopher. *Mental Processes.* Cambridge, Mass.: MIT Press, 1987.

Longuet-Higgins, Christopher, and Edward R. Lisle. "Modeling Music Cognition." *Contemporary Music Review* 3,1 (1989): 15–27.

McTear, Michael. *The Articulate Computer.* London: Basil Blackwell, 1987.

Meyer, Leonard. *Style and Music.* Philadelphia: University of Pennsylvania Press, 1989.

Pancharoen, N. "Distinguishing Musical Styles within the Romantic Era through Schenkerian Analysis." Ph. D. diss. Kent State University, November, 1985.

Pelinski, Ramon. "A Generative Grammar of Personal Eskimo Songs." *In Musical Grammars and Computer Analysis,* M. Baroni and L. Callegari, eds. Florence: Olschki, 1984.

Pereira, Fernando C. N., and David H. D. Warren. "Definite Clause Grammars for Language Analysis: A Survey of the Formalism and a Comparison with Augmented Transition Networks." *Artificial Intelligence* 13,3 (1980): 231–278.

Roads, Curtis. "An Overview of Music Representations." In *Musical Grammars and Computer Analysis,* M. Baroni and L. Callegari, eds. Florence: Olschki, 1984.

Salop, Arnold. *Studies on the History of Musical Style.* Detroit: Wayne State University Press, 1971.

Salzer, Felix. *Structural Hearing: Tonal Coherence in Music.* Vol. 2. New York: Dover Publications, 1962.

Schenker, Heinrich. *Five Analyses in Sketchform.* New York: David Mannes School of Music, 1933.

Schoenberg, Arnold. *Style and Idea*, Leonard Stein, ed. Berkeley: University of California Press, 1975.

Winograd, T. "Linguistics and the Computer Analysis of Tonal Harmony." *Journal of Music Theory* 12 (Spring 1968): 2–49.

Woods, William. "Transition Network Grammars for Natural Language Analysis." *Communications of the ACM* 13,10 (1970): 591–606.

LISP PROGRAMMING

. . . .

BASIC LISP CONCEPTS

LISP (for LISt Processing) is a symbolic programming language. It offers programmers the ability to combine small recursive functions in order to create increasingly powerful higher-level ones. This chapter is intended to serve as an introduction to LISP and its protocols. The chapter bibliography directs the reader to many sources for further study of LISP.

A simple metaphor may help in understanding the main concept behind LISP. Sulphur and carbon are fairly simple chemical elements. Postassium nitrate is a fairly simple compound. However, when a combination of 10 percent sulphur, 15 percent carbon, and 75 percent potassium nitrate is made, a substance known as gunpowder is formed. None of the elements individually gives much hint of the enormous potential of their combination. This concept represents a major LISP focus—many small functions, each doing a single job on certain types of data, when placed together in a larger function, can be used to accomplish very elegant tasks impossible for the smaller functions acting separately.

LISP Protocols

Before describing actual examples of these concepts, certain protocols of LISP must be described and understood. First, LISP requires that a function follow a left parenthesis and that all of the data it uses be followed by a right parenthesis. A program's "functions" can be defined as

```
(function-1 (function-2 (function-3 data-1)
                        (function-4 data-2)))
```

a.

```
(function-1 'a)
```

b.

```
(function-2 10)
```

c.

FIGURE 3.1   LISP protocols: a) Difference in uses of functions and data in LISP. b) The use of a single "quote" in LISP. c) The single number 10 is also an atom.

perpetrators of action. The usage of the word *function* here should not be confused with the very different usage in Chapter 2. Unfortunately, there are no adequate substitutes for either usage. Both music and computer languages have functions—they simply do not mean the same thing. In music, function is a manifestation of hierarchy. In computer jargon, a function is an operator, an expression that alters data in ways described by the function's definition. *Data,* then, refers to the atoms (non-list forms of data) and lists that are manipulated by functions. When many functions are employed, each must be closed by a right parenthesis, often causing a plethora of right parentheses, all of which must be tied to left ones. This is shown in Figure 3.1a. Here, each of the functions evaluates data or data processed by another function. That is, `function-4` acts on `data-2`, `function-3` acts on `data-1`, both of which are evaluated by `function-2`, and all of which is evaluated by `function-1`.

Second, when the first item after a left parenthesis is not a function, it should not be evaluated as one. To ensure this, LISP requires a single quote before a list as in `'(12 34 56)`. Such a list of data will not be treated as the function 12 with the data 34 and 56 but rather as a list of numbers.

Finally, LISP recognizes numbers as atoms. Letters (or contiguous groups of letters) are not atoms, except if previously defined or preceded by a quote. Therefore, 12 can stand alone as an argument (data or representations of data used by functions), while the letter a, or the word `foo`, if they are to be treated as data, must have single quotes as in `'a` and `'foo`. In Figure 3.1b and 3.1c, both `'a` and 10 are atoms.

```
(car '(48 50 52))
```

a.

```
(cdr '(48 50 52))
```

b.

```
(cons 48 '(50 52))
```

c.

```
(car (cdr '(48 50 52)))
```

d.

FIGURE 3.2 LISP primitives: a) An example of the use of car. b) An example of the use of cdr. c) A simple example of the use of cons. d) Combining functions in LISP.

LISP Primitives

With these protocols understood, one can begin to program rudimentarily in LISP. With only five primitive functions, one can give context to "words" that otherwise have little meaning and build from functions that in themselves have none. The acronym car (for "content of the address register," as used on the IBM 7090) means to retrieve or return the first element in a list used as its argument. Hence the value returned in Figure 3.2a is 48. The parentheses are rectified, and the single quote indicates that the first element in the list is not a function but data. This list contains numbers representing musical notes, with 48 as C one octave below middle C, and with each increment representing one half-step (i.e., 50 = D, etc., with the list here equaling the first three notes of the C-major scale; this pitch representation follows the integers used in the MIDI standard).

While car returns the first element of a list, cdr ("contents of the decrement register") returns the rest of the list without its first element. In Figure 3.2b, cdr produces the list (50 52).

Now, as if our activities were not banal enough, cons puts the two back together again. It does this by inserting its first argument, an atom, at the beginning of its second argument, a list. The name cons is a mnemonic for "constructor." In Figure 3.2c cons produces the list (48 50 52), and we're back to where we began. A variation of cons is append, which

takes two arguments, both of which are lists. Therefore, the code
(`append '(48) '(50 52)`) equates to (`48 50 52`). Variations of
primitive functions can be very useful, as will be seen in the next section.

The more substantial part of LISP's power originates from when these
functions combine to achieve ends that no one function in itself could
attain. Take, for example, describing a method to return the second number from the list. This is accomplished by using a combination of primitives
that we already know. Figure 3.2d produces "the first of the rest of the list."
This is because LISP evaluates functions from the data leftwards. Hence,
`cdr` is first applied, and then `car`. The LISP function `cadr` is a combination of `car` and `cdr`, allowing access to deeper nested positions in lists
with fewer parentheses. This function gets the second element of a list.
Further combinations such as `caddr` and `cadddr` (to retrieve third and
fourth elements) show how this principle can be extended. Readability,
however, becomes more and more opaque with each additional letter. It
is good to know at this point that many LISP programmers replace `car`,
`cadr`, and `cdr` with real-world English equivalents such as `first`, `sec-
ond`, and `rest`. These will be the forms used in the examples for the
remainder of this book.

LISP also provides primitives for retrieving data from the ends of lists.
The function `last`, for example, produces the last element of a list. The
call of (`last '(48 50 52)`) produces (`52`). Note the list form of the
results of using `last`, which can be very useful, as will be seen in the next
section. The opposite of this, that is, the return of a list without its last
element, is produced by the function `butlast`. The call (`butlast
'(48 50 52)`) returns (`48 50`). Both of these functions can be very
useful in working with the tails of lists.

Defining Functions in LISP

As can be seen in the previous examples, "functions"
represent generic "actors" that process actual data when they are called.
With the addition of only three more straightforward functions, a programmer can actually create new functions, name them, and use them in
performing individual tasks. This individualizes programs. What cannot be
overly stressed, however, is that new functions should always be as clean
and simple, and the function name as mnemonic, as possible.

All functions in LISP require some form of declaration. The function
`defun` (for "define function") is a LISP function for defining new functions. Each `defun` is followed by a list of argument names that will represent
data. This is followed by the body of the function, which consists of other
functions applied in various ways to the argument(s) of the function being
defined. The code in Figure 3.3a defines a new function named `second`,

```
(defun second (list-of-notes)
  (car (cdr list-of-notes)))
```

a.

```
(second '(48 50 52)) = 50
```

b.

FIGURE 3.3   a) Defining a new function in LISP. b) Using the newly created function.

```
(setq major-scale-third '(48 50 52))
```

FIGURE 3.4   The use of setq in LISP.

which takes one argument, (list-of-notes). This should be a list of numbers representing notes. The function second then returns the second member of that list. The indentation of the second line aids in readability and in rectifying parentheses. After it is defined, this function can be called as in Figure 3.3b. One need no longer write out the combination of primitives but can simply use this higher-level function.

Data Abstraction and Conditionals

The next two functions are somewhat different in nature from those just described. The function setq, short for "set quote" and pronounced "set-cue," binds data to variables. It is one method of many to abstract cumbersome lists of data during coding and running LISP encoded programs. It also represents a good example of symbol manipulation. Therefore, the code in Figure 3.4 sets major-scale-third to be (48 50 52). Thus, typing major-scale-third returns (48 50 52) — the first three notes of a major scale — and typing in (second major-scale-third) gives 50.

Finally, the simple concept of if-then-else completes a basic formulation of LISP programming techniques. The function if is a conditional that states that "if the following LISP evaluation proves true then evaluate the first expression that follows it, otherwise evaluate the second expression that follows it." This concept is shown in Figure 3.5a and an example in Figure 3.5b, in which if evaluates the test (equal 4 4), which asks "does 4 equal 4?" In this case, 4 does equal 4, so if returns 8. If one of the

```
(if some-action  [is true]
    then something
    else something-else)
```

a.

```
(if (equal 4 4) 8 9) = 8
```

b.

FIGURE 3.5   a) A description of the LISP conditional `if`.
b) Using `if`.

two 4s following `equal` had been any other number, the query would have reverted to `else` 9.

CREATING MUSIC FUNCTIONS

Now, armed with these few LISP functions, the protocols, and a few concepts such as small functions and readable code, one can begin to create rather powerful new functions that can have immediate musical applications.

Since retrograde is an often-used musical device for variation, let us attempt to create a small retrograde function from those functions already present. This will be pure exercise since the LISP function `reverse` would do the trick without the necessity of creating a new function to do it.

First, `defun` must begin the definition, as in Figure 3.6a. No single quote is necessary (`defun` is a function itself). In Figure 3.6b, the name of the function is as clear as possible. The function name is followed by a set of arguments (in this case, one) mnemonically named for the data they will ultimately represent when the function is used. This is shown in Figure 3.6c. Now, because this function will operate over and over again in order to progress through its list of arguments, it will be necessary to create an `if` statement that will notify the function when its task is accomplished. Figure 3.6d represents a start.

The function `null` evaluates to true if its argument is an empty list (also called `nil`). Therefore, in Figure 3.6e, `if` returns the evaluation of its second argument only when the argument to `retrograde` is `nil`. In the third line of Figure 3.6f, the previously defined function `append` is used

```
1.(defun
```

a.

```
1.(defun retrograde
```

b.

```
1.(defun retrograde (list-of-notes)
```

c.

```
1.(defun retrograde (list-of-notes)
2.   (if
```

d.

```
1.(defun retrograde (list-of-notes)
2.   (if (null list-of-notes)
```

e.

```
1.(defun retrograde (list-of-notes)
2.   (if (null list-of-notes) nil
3.       (append (last list-of-notes)
```

f.

```
1.(defun retrograde (list-of-notes)
2.   (if (null list-of-notes) nil
3.       (append (last list-of-notes)
4.               (retrograde (butlast list-of-notes)))))
```

g.

FIGURE 3.6   a) The first notation for defining the function
`retrograde`. b) Adding the name of the desired function.
c) The argument list in LISP. d) Location of the `if` conditional.
e) The use of `null` to inform the function when it has
completed work on its argument. f) Adding `append` to the
`retrograde` function. g) The recursive call of the function
being defined.

in the anticipation of repeated calls, each with one element removed from
the end of its argument. Note that `last` here produces the kind of first
argument required by `append`.

Finally, in Figure 3.6g, the function is complete with a recursive call of
`retrograde` with an argument trimmed of its last element by the function `butlast`. Successive calls to `retrograde` produce ever smaller

```
(retrograde '(48 50 52))
 Calling (retrograde (48 50 52))
  Calling (retrograde (48 50))
   Calling (retrograde (48))
    Calling (retrograde nil)
    retrograde returned nil
   retrograde returned (48)
  retrograde returned (50 48)
 retrograde returned (52 50 48)
(52 50 48)
```

FIGURE 3.7   A trace of the completed function `retrograde`.

(by one element) arguments until only `nil` remains. Then the conditional `if` evaluates its second argument `append` rather than its third argument.

The following represents a thumbnail sketch of what happens. Suppose `retrograde` is called with `'(48 50 52)` as its single argument. Then the list `(48 50 52)` is attached to the argument `list-of-notes`. The `if` function is called with a query "is `list-of-notes` empty?" It is not at this point, and `nil` is the return of `if`. The call to `if`'s second argument is therefore skipped as the "then" of the "if-then-else" sequence. The function `append` then binds the last element of the argument `list-of-notes`, or `(52)`, and the progression continues with the call to `retrograde`, with the last element removed (by `butlast`).

Tracing the operation of this function (that is, witnessing each call explicitly) allows observers to see each function call as shown in Figure 3.7. The indentation separates calls from returns, with the former successively moving to the right and the latter back to the left.

An interval translator makes more musical use of LISP functions. For an interval translator, the programmer requires a function that will return a list of intervals (seconds, thirds, etc.) from a list of pitches. This means simply `(2 3)` from the list `(48 50 53)`. Recursion allows for simple operations to easily process large lists such as those required for music analysis.

Figure 3.8 serves quite well for this. Before describing how this operates, the reader should observe that `second` (defined earlier) is used in Figure 3.8 instead of `(car (cdr` in order to draw upon LISP's ability to have many levels of code. Second, the empty list that follows `if`'s query to `null` indicates that the `nil` here will ultimately be the "empty list" for whatever data the `cons` in line 4 collects. This introduces a new function, "−," or the minus sign, which subtracts its second argument from its first. Therefore, `(− x y)` is equivalent in LISP to "$x - y$" in traditional

```
1.(defun interval-translator (list-of-notes)
2.   (if (null (rest list-of-notes))
3.       nil
4.       (cons
5.           (- (second list-of-notes)
6.               (first list-of-notes))
7.           (interval-translator (rest list-of-notes)))))
```

FIGURE 3.8 Definition of a function `interval-translator`, which demonstrates the use of `cons` for recursion.

mathematics, as seen in Table 3.1. In this table, each function name is followed by a list of arguments, a brief description of its purpose, and one sample run. These functions are all standard COMMON LISP primitives and can be run on any COMMON LISP implementation. Since the desired interval is the distance from the first note to the second, the first must be subtracted from the second. Negatives are possible. Indeed they are essential to describe downward motion.

This is how `interval-translator` operates (refer to Figure 3.8). As above, the function and argument names are declared. The `if` conditional again makes sure that the function doesn't recurse forever. In each call to `interval-translator`, the `cons` subtracts the first number from the second number of the list in `list-of-notes`, producing (2 3) from the input (48 50 53). Since `interval-translator` cannot create an interval from the last member of the list to `nil`, it is not necessary for the argument to be completely empty to end recursion. In fact, to do so would force an error since the "-" function cannot compute "number - nil." Hence the use of (`null` (`rest list-of-notes`)). All of the subtractions are held in the `cons` until the first evaluation of `if` is true. It then returns (2 3).

Again, the function operates cleanly and swiftly in its recursive run through its argument. Numerical representations of intervals are returned (always one less in number than the original pitch list) in a logical and economical manner. Building these functions on one another can create powerful systems whose top function can manage very complex operations.

By using a function called `mapcar`, functions can be applied to successive arguments in a list. It applies its first (function) argument to all members of its second (list) argument. In general, this avoids the creation of new functions for operations that will be required only once. For example, if one wishes to get the first element of each list in a list of lists, (`mapcar 'car list-of-lists`) will work effectively in place of a

FUNCTION	MEANING	EXAMPLE
+ <x y....>	adds all members of argument	(+ 1 3 2 4 5) = 15
− <x y....>	subtracts all y's from x	(− 8 2 3) = 3
* <x y....>	multiplies x by successive arguments	(* 1 2 3) = 6
/ <x y....>	divides x by successive arguments	(/ 4 2 1) = 2
1+ <x>	equivalent to (+ x 1)	(1+ 4) = 5
1− <x>	equivalent to (− x 1)	(1− 4) = 3

TABLE 3.1   Basic LISP mathematic functions. Note: x and y are numbers.

completely new function. Therefore, (mapcar 'car '((1 2 3)(4 5 6))) returns the list (1 4).

The function mapcar also invites the use of no-name functions. These are defined by the use of the function lambda. They are used when programmers feel the applied function is so specialized as not to warrant separate definition and name. The function inversion (shown in Figure 3.9) exemplifies this technique. Here, the function mapcar maps the internal lambda on the list-of-intervals argument, multiplying ("*" means to multiply) each in turn by −1. Hence, (1 7) becomes (−1 −7) or its inversion and (−8 −4) becomes (8 4). The call to function announces that the following expression is a temporary function. This process allows for all sorts of valuable functions to be created "on the fly," without having to clutter the environment by having them always available and named.

TOP-DOWN PROGRAMMING

The approach discussed thus far is called "bottom-up programming." This refers to the fact that functions at the lowest level are created first, then functions that use these, and then functions that use those. Bottom-up programming is a successful method for teaching the fundamentals of LISP. Programmers, however, generally prefer "top-down programming." This means creating top-level functions that describe in principle what the programmer wishes to do in terms as lucid and trans-

```
1.(defun inversion (list-of-intervals)
2.   (mapcar (function (lambda (x) (* x -1)))
3.               list-of-intervals))
```

FIGURE 3.9   Demonstration of the use of `mapcar` with a no-name function.

```
1.(defun signatures (works)
2.   (superimpose (analysis (first works))
3.                    (analysis (second works))))
```

FIGURE 3.10   Defining a top-level function that contains as yet undefined lower-level primitives.

parent as possible and then, in turn, defining functions described within the body of that top-level function. The actual data interface is the last written expression of the program. Figure 3.10, for example, might be written first. Here, the function with which to derive "signatures" (see Chapter 2) from the superimposition of analyses of two different works by the same composer is intended to produce the common patterns between the two. Neither `superimpose` nor `analysis` have yet been written at this point. Working in this manner allows programmers to produce functions in search of coding, not coding in search of function.

Top-down programming is not without its problems, however. For example, since most of the functions described at the top level do not yet exist, one cannot actually test (debug) the system until all the functions are defined. Incorrect theoretical assumptions can abound before opportunities exist to prove a program's effectiveness. This is particularly true when creating systems bound to many such assumptions. The failure of one faulty theory can easily be confused with the failure of many.

PROPERTY LISTS

Property lists represent one way to program stored data. The function `setf` shown in Figure 3.11a allows users to assign data to a given symbol. It uses the function `get` to place or replace assignments of property lists. It could store, for example, notes to a melody, as it does in Figure 3.11. What's important is that `melody` may have as many different types of attributes (such as `notes`) as desired. The code in Figure 3.11b, for example, assigns the durations to each of the pitches in the

```
(setf (get 'melody 'notes) '(48 50 53))
```

a.

```
(setf (get 'melody 'durations) '(100 50 25))
```

b.

```
(get 'melody 'durations) = (100 50 25)
(get 'melody 'notes) = (48 50 53)
```

c.

FIGURE 3.11   a) An example of a property list. b) Demonstration of how more than one indicator can be assigned to a single property list. c) Using note and duration representations in the assignment of property list values.

```
1.(defun act-on-all (function-representation data)
2.   (if (null data)
3.       nil
4.       (cons (apply function-representation
5.                    (first data))
6.             (act-on-all
7.               function-representation (rest data)))))
```

FIGURE 3.12   The use of `function` as argument.

`melody`. (The unit system for durations in this book is 50 for eighth notes, 100 for quarter notes, 200 for half notes, etc.) Now, calling each symbol's attribute in turn with `get` produces the results shown in Figure 3.11c.

Another important concept is found in the function `apply`. This allows for a function name to be created and then "applied" to its arguments. Imagine that somewhere in a function you had to use another function whose name is unknown until it appears as an argument to the function in use. Figure 3.12 serves as example. The functions already encountered are present, as is the recursive use of `cons`. The function `act-on-all` has no idea, however, what function will be "applied" to each member of the list of data that is fed to it as a second argument until `act-on-all` is used. The variable `function-representation` in Figure 3.12 *represents* the real function. Therefore, it cannot be called normally by placing it after a left parenthesis. LISP would look for a function called `function-representation` rather than the function represented by the local variable `function-representation`. We need a function like `apply`, which "applies" the actual function to the data that follows it. For example, if the function argument were `1+`, then a second argument of `'(48 50 52)` would produce `(49 51 53)`. Like `retrograde` presented earlier in this chapter, `act-on-all` is defined here for its instructive use only. The function `mapcar` would work effectively in its place, as in `(mapcar function data)`.

OTHER LISP FUNCTIONS

Table 3.2 presents functions that are needed for understanding code to be presented in the remainder of this book. It should be noted that " = " and "equal" have fundamental differences too complicated to address here. For further information, use the LISP references mentioned in the bibliography.

AN ATN GENERATOR

Using some of the functions described so far in this chapter along with the principles defined in Chapter 2 allows for the building of a small ATN generating program. Figure 3.13 describes the function `realize-atn`. This function is called with no arguments. It first sets `(setq)` the variable `count-down` to the result of `choose-one` in line 2. This latter function randomly chooses one of the elements of its list argument. As will be seen, `count-down` ensures alternate selection of linguistic "objects" and "descriptors" so that the small program will not immediately repeat itself. As well, it will signal the end of the program's operation.

The use of `apply`, in line 3, removes the lists in the retrieved lists of data and makes the result more readable by making a single list rather than lists of lists. The no-name function used by `mapcar` (line 4) translates the syntax lists created by `generate-atn` into English. When completed, `realize-atn` will return completed sentences based on the subphrases shown in Figure 2.21.

The database for this program has two parts, as shown in Figure 3.14. Symbols of the first part have the attribute `syntax`, which binds each respective symbol (i.e., `articles`, `adjectives`, etc.) to a list of those word types that may follow it. Symbols of the second part have the attribute `meaning`, which binds each respective symbol (i.e., `articles`,

FUNCTION	MEANING	EXAMPLE
`<= <x y>`	"less than or equal to" predicate	`(<= 5 6) = t`
`>= <x y>`	"greater than or equal to" predicate	`(>= 6 5) = t`
`= <x y>`	"equal" to predicate	`(= 2 2) = t`
`abs <x>`	returns "absolute" value of x	`(abs -4) = 4`
`and <tests>`	returns t if evaluations of tests are all `t`, otherwise `nil`	`(and (<= 1 2) (>= 2 1)) =t`
`assoc <arg1 arg2>`	returns first sublist from arg2 whose head is arg1	`(assoc 5 '((3 a) (4 b)(5 c))) = (5 c)`
`defvar <variable>`	used to declare system variables	`(defvar x 2) = x`
`equal <2 objects>`	tests for equality of arguments	`(equal 'one 'one) = t`
`eval <form>`	evaluates its argument	`(eval '(car '(1 2))) = 1`
`funcall <function arguments>`	applies function to many arguments	`(funcall 'cons 'a '(b c)) = (a b c)`
`length <list>`	returns length of list	`(length '(a b c)) = 3`
`let <variables-and-values applicable-code>`	sets local variables	`(let ((a 100) (b 200))(+ a b)) = 300`
`list <objects>`	lists its arguments	`(list 'a 2 '(c)) = (a 2 (c))`
`nconc <lists>`	used here to return its arguments without `null`	`(nconc '(a) () '(b)) = (a b)`
`nth <x list>`	returns the x'th (from 0) object	`(nth 3 '(a b c d e)) = d`
`nthcdr <x list>`	cdr's x times	`(nthcdr 2 '(a b c d) = (c d)`
`random <top-limit>`	returns a random integer, zero to `limit`	`(random 4) = 2`
`zerop <number>`	returns t if the number is zero	`(zerop 0) = t`

TABLE 3.2   More LISP functions. Note: t means "true." x and y refers to numbers.

```
1.(defun realize-atn nil
2.    (setq count-down (choose-one '(1 2)))
3.    (apply (function append)
4.          (mapcar
5.             '(lambda (x) (choose-one (get x 'meaning)))
6.             (generate-atn 'articles))))
```

FIGURE 3.13   A simple top-level ATN generating function.

adjectives, etc.) to a list that consists of words or phrases of their basic types. The syntax portion of this database therefore offers basic ordering rules, and the meaning attributes translate the syntax symbols into English.

The workhorse function of the realize-atn series of functions is generate-atn, shown in Figure 3.15. The function generate-atn begins with the articles argument provided by realize-atn and then, according to the built-in succession rules, continues to extend its argument until the setq'ed count-down has reached zero, where it returns a final object. Taking a close look at its operation gives a good example of how LISP provides tools for the development of expert systems. Line 2 sets the end of recursion for generate-atn (when count-down is 0) and adds (line 3) a final "object" to complete the sentence. Line 6 decrements the variable count-down if beginning in line 5 is a conjunction, the word type to which it is programmatically bound. In line 8, the argument (which after the initial run no longer represents the actual "beginning" of the generation) is captured by cons, and the function continues through choose-one to collect viable word types.

It is important to note that conjunctions is treated as a special case in that words of this type (such as *and*) generally connect sentence sub-phrases. By incrementally reducing count-down each time conjunctions appears as a word type (as in Figure 3.15, lines 5 through 7), the number of possible sub-phrases created at the end of each generation will be reduced until the sentence must end.

The progression through the use of eval in lines 12 and 14 ensures that the code that appears in the setfs of the conjunctions and descriptors will be evaluated and not treated as data. The other syntax property lists are word types and not code, which must be evaluated in order to provide a listed word type. Lines 11 through 15 can be read as: "if the current argument to generate-atn is either conjunctions or descriptors, then evaluate the property list found by using get, otherwise simply get the respective property list."

These two functions (realize-atn and generate-atn) and the small database produced the sentences in Figure 3.16 (again, without any

```
(setq count-down 1)

(setf (get 'articles 'syntax)
    '(adjectives subjects1 subjects2))
(setf (get 'adjectives 'syntax)
    '(subjects1 subjects2))
(setf (get 'subjects1 'syntax) '(composers1))
(setf (get 'subjects2 'syntax) '(composers2))
(setf (get 'composers1 'syntax) '(verbs1))
(setf (get 'composers2 'syntax) '(verbs2))
(setf (get 'verbs1 'syntax) '(conjunctions))
(setf (get 'verbs2 'syntax) '(conjunctions))
(setf (get 'conjunctions 'syntax)
    '(list 'descriptors (if (evenp count-down)
                            'objects1
                            'objects2)))
(setf (get 'descriptors 'syntax)
    '(list (if (evenp count-down)
               'objects1
               'objects2)))
(setf (get 'objects1 'syntax) '(conjunctions))
(setf (get 'objects2 'syntax) '(conjunctions))
```

```
(setf (get 'articles 'meaning)
    '((the) (this) (that)))
(setf (get 'adjectives 'meaning)
    '((dark)(beautiful)(lyrical)))
(setf (get 'subjects1 'meaning)
    '((sonata)(symphony)(concerto)))
(setf (get 'subjects2 'meaning)
    '((aria)(opera)(song)))
(setf (get 'composers1 'meaning)
    '((by mozart)(by beethoven)(by haydn)))
(setf (get 'composers2 'meaning)
    '((by bellini)(by verdi)(by puccini)))
(setf (get 'verbs1 'meaning)
    '((was easy to play)(was hard to play)))
(setf (get 'verbs2 'meaning)
    '((was hard to sing)(was a breeze to sing)))
(setf (get 'conjunctions 'meaning) '((and)))
(setf (get 'descriptors 'meaning)
    '((also)(very)(yet)))
(setf (get 'objects1 'meaning)
    '((lyrical)(sweet)))
(setf (get 'objects2 'meaning)
    '((profound)(deep)))
```

FIGURE 3.14 The two-part database for use with the function in Figure 3.13.

```
1.(defun generate-atn (beginning)
2.  (if (zerop count-down)
3.      (list 'objects1)
4.      (and
5.        (if (equal beginning 'conjunctions)
6.            (setq count-down (1- count-down))
7.            t)
8.        (cons beginning
9.              (generate-atn
10.                (choose-one
11.                  (if (equal beginning 'conjunctions)
12.                      (eval (get beginning 'syntax))
13.                      (if (equal beginning 'descriptors)
14.                          (eval (get beginning 'syntax))
15.                          (get beginning
16.                               'syntax)))))))))
```

FIGURE 3.15 An intervening function between the top level and data.

(THIS SYMPHONY BY MOZART WAS EASY TO PLAY AND LYRICAL)
(THE ARIA BY VERDI WAS HARD TO SING AND LYRICAL)
(THE DARK SYMPHONY BY MOZART WAS EASY TO PLAY AND LYRICAL)
(THAT CONCERTO BY HAYDN WAS HARD TO PLAY AND SWEET)
(THE BEAUTIFUL ARIA BY BELLINI WAS HARD TO SING AND YET
DEEP AND LYRICAL)
(THIS LYRICAL SONG BY PUCCINI WAS A BREEZE TO SING AND SWEET)
(THE SONATA BY BEETHOVEN WAS HARD TO PLAY AND LYRICAL)
(THIS SONG BY BELLINI WAS A BREEZE TO SING AND
VERY DEEP AND LYRICAL)
(THIS BEAUTIFUL SONATA BY MOZART WAS HARD TO PLAY AND
ALSO PROFOUND AND LYRICAL)
(THIS SONG BY VERDI WAS HARD TO SING AND SWEET)
(THE LYRICAL ARIA BY BELLINI WAS A BREEZE TO SING AND LYRICAL)
(THAT OPERA BY PUCCINI WAS A BREEZE TO SING AND DEEP AND LYRICAL)
(THIS LYRICAL SONG BY PUCCINI WAS A BREEZE TO SING
AND YET DEEP AND LYRICAL)
(THIS LYRICAL OPERA BY PUCCINI WAS HARD TO SING AND
ALSO PROFOUND AND SWEET)
(THIS OPERA BY VERDI WAS A BREEZE TO SING AND SWEET)
(THIS OPERA BY BELLINI WAS A BREEZE TO SING AND LYRICAL)
(THIS OPERA BY PUCCINI WAS A BREEZE TO SING AND SWEET)
(THE OPERA BY BELLINI WAS A BREEZE TO SING
AND LYRICAL)
(THIS SONATA BY MOZART WAS HARD TO PLAY AND LYRICAL)
(THE ARIA BY VERDI WAS A BREEZE TO SING AND LYRICAL)

FIGURE 3.16 Sample runs of the function `generate-atn`.

editing by the author). Compare the results of this program to Figure 2.21, in which the same words are laid out in an ATN diagram. While the limitations of such a small program (two functions with a small database) are obvious, the implications should be clear. With expansion, the ATN generating program could produce an extremely powerful program capable of responding to widely varied user needs.

BIBLIOGRAPHY

Allen, John. *Anatomy of LISP*. New York: McGraw-Hill, 1978.

Berk, A. A. *LISP: The Language of Artificial Intelligence*. London: Collins, 1985.

Foderaro, John. *The Franz LISP Manual*. Berkeley: University of California Press, 1979.

Kornfeld, William. "Machine Tongues VII." *Computer Music Journal* 4,2 (Summer 1980): 6–12.

Minsky, Marvin. *The Society of Mind*. New York: Simon and Schuster, 1986.

Siklóssy, Laurent. *Let's Talk LISP*. Englewood Cliffs, N.J.: Prentice-Hall, 1976.

Steele, Guy. *Common LISP*. Burlington, Mass.: Digital Press, 1984.

Touretzky, David. *LISP: A Gentle Introduction to Symbolic Computation*. New York: Harper and Row, 1984.

Wilensky, Robert. *Common LISPcraft*. New York: W. W. Norton, 1984.

Winston, P. H., and B. K. P. Horn. *LISP*. 2d ed. Reading, Mass.: Addison-Wesley, 1984.

STYLE REPLICATION

. . . .

AN ELEMENTARY LISP COMPOSING PROGRAM

It is now time to relate elements of various concepts covered in this book. The works chosen as examples for an elementary LISP composing program are from the Bach *15 Two-Part Inventions* (which were also used to create the new inventions shown at the beginning of Chapter 5). This chapter combines the work of Chapter 2 (usage of the SPEAC system) and Chapter 3 (LISP) and presents another principle, pattern matching, in some detail. After a discussion of the code for an elementary composing program, this chapter concludes with the presentation of two short inventions created by the program.

There are many approaches to computer replication of musical styles. For example, one could program rules about what constitutes generic musical style and then compose new music by varying code to meet the needs of particular styles (Meehan 1980 and Baroni and Callegari 1984). This method creates problems since it limits users to those who (1) can program effectively in the chosen computer language and (2) have the musical ability to convert what they define as particular styles into programmable components. Since such individuals are fairly rare, interfaces that can act as intermediaries must be built if the program is ever to have any general use. EMI has one such interface called the *style dictionary*. It consists of a series of questions (over a thousand at last count) that allow one to communicate with responses of Yes or No. These responses then control the program's choices of constraints. Figure 4.1 presents a list of some of the many parameters relevant to musical style.

1. **Ality**
   1.1. Modality
   1.2. Tonality
   1.3. Amodality, Atonality
2. **Inheritance**
   2.1. Antiquity
   2.2. Middle Ages
      2.2.1. Tradition
            Western
            Non-Western
   2.3. Renaissance
   2.4. Baroque
   2.5. Rococo
   2.6. Classic
   2.7. Romantic
   2.8. Contemporary
3. **Form**
   3.1. Key predominance
      3.1.1. key (major/minor)
      3.1.2. level of contrast between keys
      3.1.3. non-triadic (clusters, 4th-5th chords)
      3.1.4. polytonal
      3.1.5. added tones
      3.1.6. synthetic scales
   3.2. Dodecaphonic (strict/free/combinatorial)
   3.3. Expectation/fulfillment/deception
   3.4. Use of introductions
   3.5. Use of transitions
4. **Melody**
   4.1. Shape
      4.1.1. phrase balance (symmetry/antecedence–consequence)
      4.1.2. contour (arch/climactic)
   4.2. Scale
      4.2.1. relation to beat
      4.2.2. level of use
   4.3. Variation techniques (inversion/retrograde, etc.)
   4.4. Chromaticism
      4.4.1. approach (stepwise/leap)
      4.4.2. resolution (stepwise/leap)
      4.4.3. passing
      4.4.4. accented
   4.5. Cadence
      4.5.1. penultimate note (dominant/tonic)
      4.5.2. ultimate note (dominant/tonic)
5. **Harmony**
   5.1. Protocols
   5.2. Cadences

FIGURE 4.1   A sample of possibilities used to build a style dictionary.

5.2.1. predominant types
    authentic complete/incomplete
    deceptive
    half
    plagal
5.2.2. influence of location
    period ends
    section ends
    movement ends
5.3. Inversions
  5.3.1. influence of location
    cadence
    incipience
    mid-phrase
  5.3.2. use implications
    next chord
    other chords
    cadential patterns
  5.3.3. cadential 6/4
  5.3.4. cadential 6/5
  5.3.5. 6 in diminished triad
5.4. Voice leading
  5.4.1. degree resolutions
    following norm
  5.4.2. rules by voice
    top voice
    bottom voice
    inner voices
      closest member of chord
      common tone
      forced contrary motion
    doubling
      root
      fifth
      third restrictions
5.5. Chromaticism
  5.5.1. type
    secondary dominants (V/V, etc.)
    diminished sevenths
    borrowed
    ornament
      augmented sixth chords
      Neopolitan sixth chords
    modulatory
      closely related keys
        common chords
      far related keys
        sudden modulation
        respelled augmented sixth chords
        respelled diminished seventh chords

FIGURE 4.1   continued.

5.6. Harmonic rhythm
    5.6.1. common with metric type
    5.6.2. agogic accent created
5.7. Non-harmonic tones
    5.7.1. generic types (passing, neighbors, etc.)
    5.7.2. resolution delay
    5.7.3. expectation/fulfillment/deception
6. Counterpoint
    6.1. Imitation
        6.1.1. metric binds
        6.1.2. stretto
        6.1.3. strictness
    6.2. Voicing
    6.3. Hemiola
    6.4. Polyrhythm
7. Foreground
    7.1. Embellishment
        7.1.1. trills
        7.1.2. appoggiaturas
        7.1.3. turns
        7.1.4. other grace notes
    7.2. Sequence
        7.2.1. stepwise (diatonic/chromatic)
        7.2.2. cycle of fifths

FIGURE 4.1   continued.

Another way that one can build programs for the replication of musical styles is to enter into the computer some representation for the actual music of a composer. This can then be analyzed for various properties, and the information can be used to compose new works. This has the advantage that one need not be conversant with a programming language since many of the aspects of style would be captured in the composing program itself.

THE COMPOSE-INVENTION PROGRAM

The following program assumes that by pattern matching (Fu 1982) two or more melodies, one can derive signatures (see Chapter 2). New works can be created when these signatures are ordered by a SPEAC system like the one described in Chapter 2. The composing sequence occurs in the following basic steps. First, it divides each work into pitch motives and compares the results, creating a list of duplications among works (signatures). It then generates a logical arrangement of

```
(setq r 0 c1 36 c#1 37 d1 38 d#1 39 e1 40 f1 41
f#1 42 g1 43 g#1 44 a1 45 a#1 46 b1 47 c2 48 c#2
49 d2 50 d#2 51 e2 52 f2 53 f#2 54 g2 55 g#2 56
a2 57 a#2 58 b2 59 c3 60 c#3 61 d3 62 d#3 63 e3 64
f3 65 f#3 66 g3 67 g#3 68 a3 69 a#3 70 b3 71 c4 72
c#4 73 d4 74 d#4 75 e4 76 f4 77 f#4 78 g4 79 g#4 80
a4 81 a#4 82 b4 83 c5 84 c#5 85 d5 86 d#5 87 e5 88
f5 89 f#5 90 g5 91 g#5 92 a5 93 a#5 94 b5 95 c6 96)

(setq  qtr 100 eth-dot 75 eth 50 sxtnth 25)
```

FIGURE 4.2   The basic `setq`s of note names and durations for the `compose-invention` program.

SPEAC identifiers, translates the identifiers into their assigned meanings, and associates the direction of each signature with those meanings (how the direction is calculated is explained below). Finally, it pattern matches durations and arranges the motives into note and duration lists.

The first thing this signature-using composing program does is abstract data in such a way that it can be read in ways more musical than if the program were to use numbers only. Figure 4.2 shows the `setq`s of note names and durations. The actual function `setq` need not be repeated because it can sequence through data in a list by pairs, the first as the variable and the second as its value. Even though this program will be diatonic, it's a good idea to include a chromatic scale to simplify creating programs capable of dealing with chromatic materials. The list of `setq`'ed data is necessary since translation of notes will require applying a recursive function that will find the number and return its name. The same process can be applied to the lists of durations. The abbreviations are: `qtr` for quarter note, `eth-dot` for dotted eighth note, `eth` for eighth note, and `sxtnth` for sixteenth note.

With the exception of finding consonant notes for countersubjects, the program described in the following section inherits its scale from the data—hence, the results will automatically be in the same scale as the input. Figure 4.3 is a `setq` of a five-octave major scale used for creating accompanying lines and tonics for cadences in the `compose-invention` program. Creating code that will identify the tonic chord will help force the tonic into the bass. Likewise, creating code that will identify the tonic note will help force it into the bass in the final cadence. Rests of a quarter-note duration will be required during composition and are `setq`'ed here so that they will not actually appear in later functions. The data looks this way (i.e., headed by `nil`) because this is the form required

```
(setq major-scale
'(36 38 40 41 43 45 47 48 50 52 53 55 57 59 60 62 64
65 67 69 71 72 74 76 77 79 81 83 84 86 88 89 91
93 95 96))

(setq dominant
     '(43 55 67 79 91 47 59 71 83 95 50 62 74 86))

(setq tonic
     '(36 48 60 72 84 96 40 52 64 76 88 43 55
        67 79 91))

(setq tonic-note '(36 48 60 72 84 96))

(setq quarter-rest '((nil (0))(nil (100))))
```

FIGURE 4.3   The `setq` of `major-scale` for accompanying lines and tonics for cadences in the `compose-invention` program.

a.

FIGURE 4.4   The beginning of Bach's Invention No. 1. a) Score. b) Pitches. c) Pitches as numbers. d) Durations.

```lisp
(setf (get 'bach-invention-1 'pitches)
    '(r c3 d3 e3 f3 d3 e3 c3 g3 c4 b3 c4 d4 g3
a3 b3 c4 a3 b3 g3 d4 g4 f4 g4 e4 a4 g4 f4 e4 g4
f4 a4 g4 f4 e4 d4 c4 e4 d4 f4 e4 d4 c4 b3 a3 c4
b3 d4 c4 b3 a3 g3 f3 a3 g3 b3 a3 d3 c4 d4 b3 a3
g3 f3 e3 g3 f3 a3 g3 b3 a3 c4 b3 d4 c4 e4 d4 c4
d4 g4 b3 a3 g3 g3))
```

b.

```lisp
(0 60 62 64 65 62 64 60 67 72 71 72 74 67 69 71
72 69 71 67 74 79 77 79 76 81 79 77 76 79 77 81
79 77 76 74 72 76 74 77 76 74 72 71 69 72 71 74
72 71 69 67 65 69 67 71 69 62 72 74 71 69 67 65
64 67 65 69 67 71 69 72 71 74 72 76 74 72 74 79
71 69 67 67)
```

c.

```lisp
(setf (get 'bach-invention-1 'durations)
    '(sxtnth sxtnth sxtnth sxtnth sxtnth sxtnth
sxtnth sxtnth eth eth eth eth sxtnth sxtnth sxtnth
sxtnth sxtnth sxtnth sxtnth sxtnth eth eth eth eth
sxtnth sxtnth sxtnth sxtnth sxtnth sxtnth sxtnth
sxtnth sxtnth sxtnth sxtnth sxtnth sxtnth sxtnth
sxtnth sxtnth sxtnth sxtnth sxtnth sxtnth sxtnth
sxtnth sxtnth sxtnth sxtnth sxtnth sxtnth sxtnth
sxtnth sxtnth sxtnth sxtnth eth eth eth-dot sxtnth
sxtnth sxtnth sxtnth sxtnth sxtnth sxtnth sxtnth
sxtnth sxtnth sxtnth sxtnth sxtnth sxtnth sxtnth
sxtnth sxtnth sxtnth sxtnth sxtnth sxtnth eth
sxtnth sxtnth eth))
```

d.

FIGURE 4.4 continued.

by the function `rest-beats` (see Figure 4.22c and preceding discussion).

There are four program variables worth mentioning briefly here that will be described in more detail as they appear in the code examples. The use of * in this program indicates that these variables can be accessed by the user. In brief, *size* (initialized to 3) is the size of the motives for signature gathering; *variance* (set to 1) represents the allowable amount by which a given interval may be incorrect during pattern matching; *rough-phrase-length* (initialized to 6) crudely determines the maximum length of SPEAC generation; and *minimum-length*

a.

FIGURE 4.5   The beginning of Bach's Invention No. 5. a) Score.
b) Pitches. c) Pitches as numbers. d) Durations.

(set to 5) is the minimum length of an invention before a cadence can
occur. This ensures that the composition will not simply begin and cadence immediately thereafter.

To replicate a given style, two or more simple melodies in the style are
necessary. The reader is encouraged to examine the works by Bach in
Figures 4.4 and 4.5 in order to observe actions of the functions on that
data. The music is in two parts (full score), but the note lists contain
information only about the top voice. The score is included to give readers
who are not familiar with the style of inventions an opportunity to observe
it. Briefly, inventions are short two-part works for keyboard with high
levels of offset imitation between voices and with (usually) contrasting

```
(setf (get 'bach-invention-5 'pitches)
    '(r c3 b2 c3 d3 e3 f3 r d3 c3 d3 e3 f3 g3 e3
a3 g3 f3 e3 f3 g3 f3 e3 d3 c3 e3 g3 c4 c4 a3 b3 c4
d4 c4 b3 c4 b3 a3 b3 c4 a3 b3 g3 g4 f4 g4 e4 f4 d4
e4 c4 e3 d3 e3 c3 d3 b2 c3 a2 g3 f3 e3 f3 g3 e3 f3
g2 g3 f3 e3 f3 g3 e3 f3 d3 g3 f3 e3 d3 e3 c3 d3 b2
e3 d3 c3 b2 c3 a2 b2 d2 c3 b2 a2 b2 c3 a2 b2 c3))
```

b.

```
(0 60 59 60 62 64 65 0 62 60 62 64 65 67 64 69 67
65 64 65 67 65 64 62 60 64 67 72 72 69 71 72 74 72
71 72 71 69 71 72 69 71 67 79 77 79 76 77 74 76 72
64 62 64 60 62 59 60 57 67 65 64 65 67 64 65 55 67
65 64 65 67 64 65 62 67 65 64 62 64 60 62 59 64 62
60 59 60 57 59 50 60 59 57 59 60 57 59 60)
```

c.

```
(setf (get 'bach-invention-5 'durations)
    '(eth sxtnth sxtnth eth eth qtr qtr eth sxtnth
sxtnth eth eth qtr qtr eth eth eth eth sxtnth sxtnth
sxtnth sxtnth eth eth eth eth eth eth sxtnth sxtnth
sxtnth sxtnth eth eth sxtnth sxtnth sxtnth sxtnth
sxtnth sxtnth sxtnth sxtnth sxtnth sxtnth sxtnth
sxtnth sxtnth sxtnth sxtnth sxtnth sxtnth sxtnth
sxtnth sxtnth sxtnth sxtnth sxtnth sxtnth sxtnth
sxtnth sxtnth sxtnth sxtnth sxtnth sxtnth sxtnth
sxtnth sxtnth sxtnth sxtnth sxtnth sxtnth sxtnth
sxtnth sxtnth sxtnth sxtnth sxtnth sxtnth sxtnth
sxtnth sxtnth sxtnth sxtnth sxtnth sxtnth sxtnth
sxtnth sxtnth sxtnth sxtnth sxtnth sxtnth sxtnth
sxtnth sxtnth sxtnth sxtnth eth))
```

d.

FIGURE 4.5   continued.

material occurring at simultaneous points. For another example of the two-part invention style, see Figure 5.2.

The lists of notes and durations for the upper voices are set as property lists using the function setf. The data in the pitch and duration lists are less readable than music, at least for musicians, and yet more readable than lists of numbers only (i.e., it is easier to identify "B3" as B natural than it is to identify "71" as B natural). One would still prefer actual music notation as a standard interface, but that is not feasible with this small program. There are differences between the notated works and the note

FUNCTION	MEANING	EXAMPLE
cond <tests>	Evaluates arg following first of the tests that returns t	(cond ((= 1 2) nil) ((= 1 1) t)) = t
function <lambda expression>	used before functions used as arguments	(mapcar (function plusp) '(1 -2 3)) = (t nil t)
make-list <x elements>	gives an x lengthed list of repeated elements	(make-list 2 :initial-element 'y) = (y y)
member <object list>	returns sub-list of list beginning with object if object is a member of list	(member 'a '(b a c)) = (a c)
minusp <x>	returns t if x is negative	(minusp -4) = t (minusp 3) = nil

TABLE 4.1   More functions for use in the compose-invention program.

lists. The note lists have been laundered of accidentals because this program would have severe cross-relations and chromatic dissonances if the accidentals were present. For the sake of simplicity, trills and some other ornamentation have been omitted in these two examples. Also, the data in Figure 4.5 have also been altered from the original music in that the note lists are in C major, whereas the original music is in E♭ major.

Compose-Invention

Table 4.1 presents five more primitive LISP functions necessary to build this particular program. Some of them are variations of previously learned functions. For example, cond is a complex if type function. Knowledge of the operation of these and the functions presented in Chapter 3 is necessary for the understanding of the program that follows.

Figure 4.6 shows the major top-level function of the compose-invention program. It will create small two-part inventions similar in nature (not in quality) to those created by Bach. The function compose-invention will use the notation of Figure 4.4c. Functions will be generally discussed as they are encountered in compose-invention, and their sub-functions will be shown before new code in compose-invention is revealed. Hence, the presentation is not always hierarchical. Utility

```
1.(defun compose-invention (composition-1 composition-2)
2.    (setq meter (select-meter))
3.    (setq prepared-data
4.            (prepare-data composition-1 composition-2))
5.    (setq signature-dictionary (find-patterns))
6.    (setq melody (make-melody))
7.    (setq initial-new-composition (add-second-voice))
8.    (setq invention (cadence-it)))

#|
(compose-invention 'bach-invention-1
                   'bach-invention-5)
(((71) (100)) ((0) (100)))
(((69 72 72 71) (25 25 25 25)) ((0) (100)))
|#
```

FIGURE 4.6   The function `compose-invention`.

functions used by many different functions are reserved for the last section, as are two inventions created by this program.

The function `compose-invention` takes two arguments, which are the names of stored compositions. The first thing `compose-invention` does is randomly select duple or triple meter (Figure 4.6, line 2). It changes the note names into numbers with `prepare-data` (line 4). At this point, it prepares the composition data for pattern matching by making lists of motives the length of `*size*` and heading them with their interval content through the use of the function `prepare`.

From this point on, there are four basic levels in `compose-invention`: (1) creating a signature dictionary by pattern matching (line 5); (2) composing a simple melody of patterns and adding durations to that melody (line 6); (3) creating a second line while altering the melody and the new line to meet the imitation requirements of an invention form (line 7); and (4) providing a cadence for the new composition (line 8). Note that `setq` is used for most of these sections. This will enable users to view the data at the various levels after composing has been completed for better understanding of the inner workings of the program.

Until this point, functions have been rather simple. At this juncture, however, they will become complex, and it will be necessary to introduce a more traditional form of LISP presentation known as *pretty printing*. This form of printing a function attempts to make major points in the code more readable by providing plenty of white space and procedural indenting. This is particularly useful in functions like `get-beat` (see Figure 4.10b) and `make-melody` (Figure 4.15).

Moreover, many function descriptions will be followed by one or more runs of that function during the creation of new compositions. These are delineated by # I at the beginning and I # at the end, which clearly separates them from the actual code and is a useful Common LISP technique for not evaluating the data so enclosed. If only ". . ." occurs on an otherwise blank line, further calls of a function have not been printed to save space.

In creating the function `compose-invention`, I have attempted to follow many important coding practices as well. First, each function has been named to demonstrate as clearly as possible what it does. Second, function definitions have as little data as possible. Functions are best kept free from data so that they can remain as flexible as possible. Third, functions are generally short, doing specific operations in specific ways. All of these practices will, I hope, help the first-time reader of the code to understand the rationale of the program.

Translation Functions

The function `select-meter`, shown in Figure 4.7a, provides the program with a choice of duple or triple meter in the form of either 2 or 3. The function `select-meter` abstracts data for the top level. It chooses a meter, which is then passed to many of the lower-level composition functions. (The function `choose-one` is shown in Figure 4.17c.)

Figure 4.7b presents the code for `prepare-data` (used in Figure 4.6, line 4), which uses `change-into-numbers` to create temporary storage locations for compositions represented as numbers instead of symbols. The variables `temporary-composition-1` and `temporary-composition-2` can then be accessed without altering the setf'ed data of Figures 4.4 and 4.5. The function `prepare-data` alters the numerical data (by using the function `prepare`) at the beginning of the composition process.

Figure 4.8 shows `change-into-numbers`, a function for converting the note and duration names of the works being replicated. This is an iterative (non-recursive) function that evaluates its arguments through a `mapcar` of `eval`. As mentioned earlier, since we don't want to alter the data in the `setf` itself, the data is placed in temporary containers for storage (e.g., `temporary-composition-1`). Therefore the data in the actual work name location remains user-readable, and the data in the temporary storage is readable by the functions. Note that the function returns the result of the last `setf`—a list of translated duration representations.

```
1.(defun select-meter nil (choose-one '(2 3)))

#|
 Calling (select-meter)
 select-meter returned 3
 |#
```

a.

```
1.(defun prepare-data (work-1 work-2)
2.   (change-into-numbers work-1 work-2)
3.   (prepare 'temporary-composition-1
4.            'temporary-composition-2
5.            'pitches))

#|
 Calling (prepare-data bach-invention-1
                       bach-invention-5)
 prepare-data returned
  ((((60 2 2) (0 60 62 64))
    ((-3 2 -4) (65 62 64 60))
    ((5 -1 1) (67 72 71 72))
    ((-7 2 2) (74 67 69 71))
    ((-3 2 -4) (72 69 71 67)) ...)
   (((60 -1 1) (0 60 59 60))
    ((2 1 -65) (62 64 65 0))
    ((-2 2 2) (62 60 62 64))
    ((2 -3 5) (65 67 64 69))
    ((-2 -1 1) (67 65 64 65)) ...))
 |#
```

b.

FIGURE 4.7   a) The function `select-meter` with a sample run. It is found in line 2 of `compose-invention`. b) The function `prepare-data` first changes the note names into numbers and then uses `prepare` to organize the data for composition.

Prepare

In Figure 4.9, the function `prepare` applies the function `mapcar` with a no-name function onto the databases. Note the use of `function` here. It declares that what follows is a function and allows that function to have access to the arguments given to `prepare`. It is generally a good idea to use `function` for consistency even when not accessing arguments. In the call to `get`, `type` refers to pitches or durations and `composition-1` and `composition-2` refer to composition names. The function `make-lists`, as will be seen in Figure 4.11, segments the database into motives the length of *size*. Then `translate` converts

```
1.(defun change-into-numbers (composition-1 composition-2)
2.  (setf (get 'temporary-composition-1 'pitches)
3.        (mapcar 'eval (get composition-1 'pitches)))
4.  (setf (get 'temporary-composition-1 'durations)
5.        (mapcar 'eval (get composition-1 'durations)))
6.  (setf (get 'temporary-composition-2 'pitches)
7.        (mapcar 'eval (get composition-2 'pitches)))
8.  (setf (get 'temporary-composition-2 'durations)
9.        (mapcar 'eval (get composition-2 'durations))))
```

```
#|
 Calling (change-into-numbers bach-invention-1
                              bach-invention-5)
 change-into-numbers returned (50 25 25 50 50 ...)
|#
```

FIGURE 4.8 The function change-into-numbers with a sample run. It is found in line 2 of prepare-data.

```
1.(defun prepare (composition-1 composition-2 type)
2.  (mapcar
3.    (function
4.      (lambda (work-name)
5.        (translate
6.          (if (equal type 'pitches)
7.              (make-lists (get work-name type) *size*)
8.              (get-beats (get work-name type)))
9.          type)))
10.  (list composition-1 composition-2)))
```

```
#|
Calling (prepare temporary-composition-1 temporary-
composition-2 pitches)
prepare returned
 ((((60 2 2) (0 60 62 64))
   ((-3 2 -4) (65 62 64 60))
   ((5 -1  1) (67 72 71 72))
   ((-7 2 2) (74 67 69 71))
   (-3 2 -4) (72 69 71 67))...)
  (((60 -1 1) (0 60 59 60))
   ((2 1 -65) (62 64 65 0))
   ((-2 2 2) (62 60 62 64))
   ((2 -3  5) (65 67 64 69))
   ((-2 -1 1) (67 65 64 65))...))
```

FIGURE 4.9 The function prepare, found in line 3 of prepare-data (Figure 4.7b).

these lists into intervals (if the argument `type` is `pitches`) or relationships (if the argument `type` is `durations`). Finally, `mapcar` maps these functions on each composition `list`'ed (line 7) so as to be in the single list-of-lists argument required by `mapcar`.

This function prepares the `*size*`'ed motives for SPEAC and pattern matching by prefacing motives with their intervals. Since the length of the motives is determined by the global variable `*size*`, altering the default value allows for matching smaller or larger motives. The larger a motive is, the less likely matches will be found. At the same time, when two larger motives match, a resulting work would sound more like one or more of the actual compositions in the database. In contrast, the smaller the motive, the more likely matches will be found and the more diverse the new compositions become. Two pitches are the limit since one note would not produce an interval for the matching process. The name `temporary-composition-1` in Figure 4.7b refers to a location where works are stored. But it is no longer necessary to know that this data is temporary, so more logical names like `composition-1` can be used.

The function run in Figure 4.9 shows the results of a call to `prepare`. It uses `pitches` as a third argument, so lists of two lists are returned. The first of these ("`(60 2 2)`") represents the three intervals in the four notes of the second list ("`(0 60 62 64)`") . This procedure is based on a use of `interval-translator`, given in Figure 3.8. This will later allow matches such as (84 83 84) to (78 77 78) as both are (−1 1) when represented as intervals. In runs that use `durations` as the third argument, the first list will be the result of dividing each duration by the next duration in the list. This represents a scaling process that allows for matches of types of rhythms. For example, quarter-eighth-eighth will match eighth-sixteenth-sixteenth since they are both (2 1) proportionally. (The run shown for Figure 4.9 is identical to the output for Figure 4.7b since Figure 4.7b returns the call to `prepare`.)

The functions `get-beats` and `get-beat` (shown respectively in Figures 4.10a and 4.10b) return duration lists grouped by beats. Beats are accumulated until their sum reaches 100, which represents a quarter note. The last line of the sample run in Figure 4.10a shows the final result of processing the upper line of the Bach Invention No. 1. (The same is true in Figures 4.11 and 4.12a.) At this point it is not possible also to form connecting note lists into beat-sized patterns because they have been collected according to the `*size*` variable into lists for pattern matching.

The function `make-lists`, shown in Figure 4.11, is used by `prepare` and does exactly what its name implies: makes its list argument into lists the length of its `length` argument. The function `firstn` returns a list of

```
1.(defun get-beats (durations)
2.  (if (<= (apply '+ durations) 100)
3.      (list durations)
4.      (let ((beat (get-beat durations 0)))
5.        (cons beat
6.              (get-beats
7.                (nthcdr (length beat) durations)))))))

#|
 Calling (get-beats (25 25 25 25 25 ...))
  Calling (get-beats (25 25 25 25 50 ...))
   Calling (get-beats (50 50 50 50 25 ...))
    Calling (get-beats (50 50 25 25 25 ...))
     Calling (get-beats (25 25 25 25 25 ...))
      Calling (get-beats (25 25 25 25 50 ...))
       Calling (get-beats (50 50 50 50 25 ...))
        ...
      get-beats returned ((25 25 25 25) (25 25 25 25)
        (50 50) (50 50) (25 25 25 25) ...)
     get-beats returned ((50 50) (25 25 25 25)
       (25 25 25 25) (50 50) (50 50) ...)
    get-beats returned ((50 50) (50 50) (25 25 25 25)
      (25 25 25 25) (50 50) ...)
   get-beats returned ((25 25 25 25) (50 50) (50 50)
     (25 25 25 25) (25 25 25 25) ...)
  get-beats returned ((25 25 25 25) (25 25 25 25) (50 50)
    (50 50) (25 25 25 25) ...)
 |#
```

                    a.

FIGURE 4.10   a) The function get-beats, found in line 8 of
prepare (Figure 4.9). b) The function get-beat, found in line
4 of get-beats.

cars of its second argument to its first argument's depth. The use of
make-lists is classically recursive in that it simply accumulates successive cars of its first argument until the conditional is met. This happens
when the first argument is null beyond the nthcdr of the second
argument.

The function translate, shown in Figure 4.12a, operates interval-
translator, defined in Figure 3.8, or duration-translator,
depending on whether it has been called with pitches or durations. As
noted earlier, pitches used as an argument begins each returned list
with a list of intervals. It is important that *both* interval and pitch information be returned by translate. As will be seen, retaining note and
duration lists is very important for the translation of matched motives back

```
1.(defun get-beat (durations beat-update)
2.  (cond ((= beat-update 100)
3.          nil)
4.          ((> (+ beat-update (first durations)) 100)
5.          (get-beat
6.            (append
7.              (make-list 2
8.                          :initial-element
9.                          (/ (first durations) 2))
10.             durations)
11.           beat-update))
12.         (t
13.          (cons (first durations)
14.                (get-beat (rest durations)
15.                          (+ beat-update
16.                             (first durations)))))))))
```

```
#|
 Calling (get-beat (25 25 25 25 25 ...) 0)
  Calling (get-beat (25 25 25 25 25 ...) 25)
   Calling (get-beat (25 25 25 25 25 ...) 50)
    Calling (get-beat (25 25 25 25 25 ...) 75)
     Calling (get-beat (25 25 25 25 50 ...) 100)
     get-beat returned nil
    get-beat returned (25)
   get-beat returned (25 25)
  get-beat returned (25 25 25)
 get-beat returned (25 25 25 25)
|#
```

b.

FIGURE 4.10 continued.

to their real pitch representations. The function `duration-translator`, shown in Figure 4.12b, divides successive pairs (in lines 5 and 6) of its argument (`list-of-durations`). This allows matches of fractionally equivalent rhythms.

Pattern-match

Figure 4.13 contains the entire pattern-match series of functions. The function `find-patterns`, called from line 5 of Figure 4.6, represents the top level of this part of the presentation and appears in Figure 4.13a. The function `pattern-match`, shown in Figure 4.13b, separates its single list argument into two arguments for `match`.

The function `match`, shown in Figure 4.13c, takes the lists of one database provided by `prepare` (Figure 4.9) and recursively applies them

```
1.(defun make-lists (notes-or-durations length-of-lists)
2.   (if (null (nthcdr length-of-lists notes-or-durations))
3.       nil
4.       (cons (firstn length-of-lists notes-or-durations)
5.             (make-lists
6.               (nthcdr length-of-lists notes-or-durations)
7.               length-of-lists))))

#|
 Calling (make-lists (0 60 62 64 65 ...) 4)
  Calling (make-lists (65 62 64 60 67 ...) 4)
   Calling (make-lists (67 72 71 72 74 ...) 4)
    Calling (make-lists (74 67 69 71 72 ...) 4)
     Calling (make-lists (72 69 71 67 74 ...) 4)
      ...
       make-lists returned ((72 69 71 67) (74 79 77 79)
        (76 81 79 77) (76 79 77 81) (79 77 76 74) ...)
       make-lists returned ((74 67 69 71) (72 69 71 67)
        (74 79 77 79) (76 81 79 77) (76 79 77 81) ...)
      make-lists returned ((67 72 71 72) (74 67 69 71)
       (72 69 71 67) (74 79 77 79) (76 81 79 77) ...)
     make-lists returned ((65 62 64 60) (67 72 71 72)
      (74 67 69 71) (72 69 71 67) (74 79 77 79) ...)
    make-lists returned ((0 60 62 64) (65 62 64 60)
     (67 72 71 72) (74 67 69 71) (72 69 71 67) ...)
 |#
```

FIGURE 4.11 The function `make-lists`, found in line 7 of `prepare` (Figure 4.9).

through a second database. The use of `nconc` (Figure 4.13c, line 4) is quite important here. It removes `nil` from its argument; hence, only matches appear in its output. This is critical since the adding that must occur later in the process would force an error if a `nil` existed in the matched data. The data input to this run is identical to the output of the run in Figure 4.7b (and Figure 4.9). No run is shown for Figure 4.13b since its output is identical to the output of Figure 4.13c.

The function `get-patterns`, shown in Figure 4.13d, is invoked by `match` and takes a single motive from the first work in the database and compares it to all of the motives in the second work to see if there is a match. If one occurs, it returns the single motive. Again, the use of intervals instead of pitches for matching is critical here. By changing the non-matching interval lists (79 77 76 74) and (67 65 64 62) into intervals (-2 -1 -2), they are properly matched.

```
1.(defun translate (notes-or-durations translation-type)
2.   (if (null notes-or-durations)
3.       nil
4.       (let ((notes (first notes-or-durations)))
5.         (cons
6.           (list
7.             (if (equal translation-type 'pitches)
8.                 (interval-translator notes)
9.                 (duration-translator notes))
10.             notes)
11.           (translate (rest notes-or-durations)
12.                      translation-type)))))

#|
 Calling (translate ((0 60 62 64) (65 62 64 60)
  (67 72 71 72) (74 67 69 71) (72 69 71 67) ...) pitches)
  Calling (translate ((65 62 64 60) (67 72 71 72)
   (74 67 69 71) (72 69 71 67) (74 79 77 79) ...) pitches)
   Calling (translate ((67 72 71 72) (74 67 69 71)
    (72 69 71 67) (74 79 77 79) (76 81 79 77) ...) pitches)
    ...
 translate returned
  (((5 -1 1) (67 72 71 72))
   ((-7 2 2) (74 67 69 71))
   ((-3 2 -4) (72 69 71 67))
   ((5 -2 2) (74 79 77 79)) (5 -2 2) (76 81 79 77)) ...)
 translate returned
  (((-3 2 -4) (65 62 64 60))
   ((5 -1 1) (67 72 71 72))
   ((-7 2 2) (74 67 69 71))
   ((-3 2 -4) (72 69 71 67))
   ((5 -2 2) (74 79 77 79)) ...)
 translate returned
  (((60 2 2) (0 60 62 64))
   ((-3 2 -4) (65 62 64 60))
   ((5 -1 1) (67 72 71 72))
   ((-7 2 2) (74 67 69 71))
   ((-3 2 -4) (72 69 71 67)) ...)
|#
```

a.

FIGURE 4.12 a) The function translate, found in line 5 of prepare (Figure 4.9). b) The function duration-translator, found in line 9 of translate.

```
1.(defun duration-translator (list-of-durations)
2.   (if (null (rest list-of-durations))
3.       nil
4.       (cons
5.          (/ (first list-of-durations)
6.             (second list-of-durations))
7.          (duration-translator
8.             (rest list-of-durations)))))

#|
 Calling (duration-translator (25 25 25 25))
  Calling (duration-translator (25 25 25))
   Calling (duration-translator (25 25))
    Calling (duration-translator (25))
    duration-translator returned nil
   duration-translator returned (1)
  duration-translator returned (1 1)
 duration-translator returned (1 1 1)
 |#
```

b.

FIGURE 4.12   continued.

The function `match-pattern`, shown in Figure 4.13e, is the actual matching function of the program. It produces `t` or `nil` depending on whether its two list arguments match within the limits allowed by the variable `*variance*`. The actual test takes place in lines 4 through 6, where each member of the second list is in turn subtracted from the parallel member of the first list and the "absolute value" compared to `*variance*`. If each is equal to or less than the allowable amount, the patterns match.

The function `directions`, shown in Figure 4.14, adds each list of intervals in its argument in order to determine the direction (positive or negative) of the motive and the severity of that direction. Thus (1 3 -2) equals 2 and (-2 -2 4) is 0. These single digits, which represent the directional thrust of a motive, are added to the head of each list so that the data is in the form shown in the single run of Figure 4.14. From right to left (the LISP order of evaluation) this is notes, intervals, and direction.

Make-melody and Generate-speac

Figure 4.15 presents the code for the high-level function `make-melody`, called from line 6 of `compose-invention` (Figure 4.6). It operates the SPEAC branch of the `compose-invention` program and accesses the `signature-dictionary` (created in line 5 of

```
1.(defun find-patterns nil
2.   (directions (pattern-match prepared-data))))
```

```
#|
 Calling (find-patterns)
 find-patterns returned
  ((5 ((3 -2 4) (76 79 77 81)))
   (-5 ((-2 -1 -2) (79 77 76 74)))
   (-5 ((-2 -2 -1) (76 74 72 71)))
   (-5 ((-1 -2 -2) (72 71 69 67)))
   (-6 ((-2 -2 -2) (71 69 67 65))) ...)
 |#
```

a.

```
1.(defun pattern-match (prepared-works)
2.   (match (first prepared-works)
3.          (second prepared-works)))
```

b.

FIGURE 4.13   The pattern-match sequence. a) The function find-patterns operates the two major functions of pattern matching: directions and pattern-match. b) The function pattern-match, found in line 2 in find-patterns. c) The function match, found in line 2 of pattern-match. d) The function get-patterns, found in line 5 of match. e) The function match-pattern, found in line 4 of get-patterns.

Figure 4.6), using associate and generate-speac to define crudely a non-metric melody. The process depends on the weighting provided by the function directions (line 6) and resultant associations (line 3) with the output of generate-speac. This melody is then given a set of beat-related durations (create-rhythms in line 12) that are the result of a less rigorous pattern-matching process (see lines 13 through 16). This pattern matching for duration parallels the structure of the pattern matching for pitches.

Figure 4.16 presents the basic syntax of the SPEAC generating program. The lexicon first presents lists of what can follow what. As was the case in Figure 3.14, the syntax attributes provide the protocol rules for the arrangement of identifiers. The lists immediately following the identifier names in each line are those identifiers that can legally follow the one being defined. In this way, the rules of musical succession are established.

The meaning attributes then provide interval dimensions, which will be evaluated from their names after proper lists of identifiers have been generated. The intervals in Figure 4.16 represent the directions of motives

```
1.(defun match (prepared-work-1 prepared-work-2)
2.  (if (null prepared-work-1)
3.      nil
4.      (nconc
5.        (get-patterns (first prepared-work-1)
6.                             prepared-work-2)
7.        (match (rest prepared-work-1)
8.               prepared-work-2)))))
```

```
#|
Calling (match
  (((60 2 2) (0 60 62 64))
   ((-3 2 -4) (65 62 64 60))
   ((5 -1 1) (67 72 71 72))
   ((-7 2 2) (74 67 69 71))
   ((-3 2 -4) (72 69 71 67)) ...)
  (((60 -1 1) (0 60 59 60))
   ((2 1 -65) (62 64 65 0))
   ((-2 2 2) (62 60 62 64))
   ((2 -3 5) (65 67 64 69))
   ((-2 -1 1) (67 65 64 65)) ...))
   ...
 match returned
  (((3 -2 4) (76 79 77 81))
   ((-2 -1 -2) (79 77 76 74))
   ((-2 -2 -1) (76 74 72 71))
   ((-1 -2 -2) (72 71 69 67))
   ((-2 -2 -2) (71 69 67 65)) ...)
|#
```

c.

FIGURE 4.13   continued.

or potential signatures as calculated in Figure 4.14 and are not actual intervals per se. The choices follow the general principle that severe leaping (in this case a major third across a motive) asks questions (a), lesser motion (a minor third) responds to these questions (c), stationary motives are stable (s), and both (p) and (e) are the same as (a) and (c) respectively but to different degrees. These choices represent one of the author's own aesthetic judgments and are not the result of any body of evidence. Many general precepts of melodic shaping do tend to follow the notion that using *direction* is one way to create balance in music.

Figure 4.17a shows generate-speac, a variation of generate-atn, described in Figure 3.15. It produces a list of correctly generated identifiers based on the property lists shown setf'ed in Figure 4.16. In

```
1.(defun get-patterns (one-pattern many-patterns)
2.   (cond ((null many-patterns)
3.           nil)
4.          ((match-pattern (first one-pattern)
5.                          (first-of-first many-patterns))
6.           (list one-pattern))
7.          (t
8.            (get-patterns one-pattern
9.                          (rest many-patterns)))))) 

#|
 Calling (get-patterns
   ((-2 -1 -2) (79 77 76 74))
   (((-2 -1 1) (67 65 64 65))
   ((-2 -1 -2) (67 65 64 62))
   ((4 3 5) (60 64 67 72))
   ((-3 2 1) (72 69 71 72))
   ((-2 -1 1) (74 72 71 72))))
 Calling (get-patterns
   ((-2 -1 -2) (79 77 76 74))
   (((-2 -1 -2) (67 65 64 62))
   ((4 3 5) (60 64 67 72))
   ((-3 2 1) (72 69 71 72))
   ((-2 -1 1) (74 72 71 72))))
 get-patterns returned
   (((-2 -1 -2) (79 77 76 74)))
 get-patterns returned
   (((-2 -1 -2) (79 77 76 74)))
   (((-2 -1 -2) (79 77 76 ...)))
 |#
```

d.

FIGURE 4.13   continued.

other words, generate-speac creates a new melodic backbone, the structure of which follows the rules of Figure 4.16. The program variable *rough-phrase-length*, shown in line 3, operates exactly like con-junctions in Figure 3.15. In this case the higher the number, the longer the resultant phrase.

The function get-speac, shown in Figure 4.17b, selects successors to the syntax property lists as shown in line 6. The initial call to this function is randomly chosen in line 2 of Figure 4.17a. The function choose-one, described in Figure 4.17c, chooses one of the elements in the list of possible successors to the speac-character argument, thus ensuring proper protocol (see line 6 of Figure 4.17b). This is then bound

```
1.(defun match-pattern (pattern-1 pattern-2)
2.   (cond ((or (null pattern-1) (null pattern-2))
3.          t)
4.         ((<= (abs
5.                (- (first pattern-1) (first pattern-2)))
6.              *variance*)
7.           (match-pattern (rest pattern-1)
8.                          (rest pattern-2)))
9.         (t
10.          nil)))
```

```
#|
 Calling (match-pattern (-2 -1 -2) (-2 -1 1))
  Calling (match-pattern (-1 -2) (-1 1))
   Calling (match-pattern (-2) (1))
   match-pattern returned nil
  match-pattern returned nil
 match-pattern returned nil
 Calling (match-pattern (-2 -1 -2) (-2 -1 -2))
  Calling (match-pattern (-1 -2) (-1 -2))
   Calling (match-pattern (-2) (-2))
    Calling (match-pattern nil nil)
    match-pattern returned t
   match-pattern returned t
  match-pattern returned t
 match-pattern returned t
|#
```

e.

FIGURE 4.13   continued.

to cons, and the function recurses. If the identifier is an a, the end–number argument is decremented just as in generate-atn with count–down (again see Figure 3.15). This allows the phrase eventually to end (see line 2). Finally, get–speac ensures a consequent motion by the addition of a final c in line 3.

The function choose-one in Figure 4.17c selects one of the members of its list argument based on the LISP function random. It is also used in, for example, select-meter (Figure 4.7a) to choose between several correct possibilities. The function random assumes that it will be selecting a number from the range of 0 to the number provided in its argument. Calling make-random-state (a standard Common LISP function) with t as a second argument to random ensures as close to pure random output as possible.

The first step in explaining how the meanings of Figure 4.16 are related to signatures is given in Figure 4.18a, which shows the function find–it.

```
1.(defun directions (signatures)
2.  (if (null signatures)
3.      nil
4.      (cons
5.        (list
6.          (apply (function +)
7.                   (first-of-first signatures))
8.            (first signatures))
9.          (directions (rest signatures)))))

#|
Calling (directions
  (((3 -2 4) (76 79 77 81))
   ((-2 -1 -2) (79 77 76 74))
   ((-2 -2 -1) (76 74 72 71))
   ((-1 -2 -2) (72 71 69 67))
   ((-2 -2 -2) (71 69 67 65))) ...))
        ...
  directions returned
   ((5 ((3 -2 4) (76 79 77 81)))
    (-5 ((-2 -1 -2) (79 77 76 74)))
    (-5 ((-2 -2 -1) (76 74 72 71)))
    (-5 ((-1 -2 -2) (72 71 69 67)))
    (-6 ((-2 -2 -2) (71 69 67 65))) ...)
 |#
```

FIGURE 4.14   The function directions, found in line 2 of find-patterns (Figure 4.13a).

This function tests to see if the direction of successive cars of signatures is in the list of meanings, its first argument. If the test is successful, then find-it returns the intervals and notes it finds in the second-of-first (see line 7) part of its second argument. Otherwise, find-it recurses through the remainder of its second argument.

When find-it relates the direction of a motive with the meaning, it divests both arguments of their signs through the use of abs (line 5). This equates downward motives (i.e., negatives) with upward ones that have the same degree of overall leap. This may seem peculiar since the two meanings given to the SPEAC symbols become the same at this point. This is necessitated, however, by the need to find signatures in small works for examples in this book. The longer the compositions used for signature analysis, the more flexible and useful the SPEAC system becomes. The meanings, for example, could be ranges, different numbers, and so forth, any of which would be effective when using larger *size* numbers or compositions that leap more than those included here. A larger system

```
1.(defun make-melody nil
2.  (let ((melody
3.          (associate (generate-speac)
4.                     (if signature-dictionary
5.                         signature-dictionary
6.                         (directions
7.                          (funcall
8.                           (choose-one
9.                            '(first second))
10.                           prepared-data))))))
11.    (list melody
12.          (create-rhythms
13.           (pattern-match
14.            (prepare 'temporary-composition-1
15.                     'temporary-composition-2
16.                     'durations))
17.          (get-length melody)))))
```

```
#|
  Calling (make-melody)
  make-melody returned
   (((((-2 -1 -2) (79 77 76 74))
     ((-2 -1 -2) (79 77 76 74))
     ((-2 -2 -1) (76 74 72 71))
     ((-2 -2 -1) (76 74 72 71))
     ((-2 -1 -2) (79 77 76 74)) ...)
    (((1 1 1) (25 25 25 25))
     ((1 1 1) (25 25 25 25))
     ((1 1 1) (25 25 25 25))
     ((1 1 1) (25 25 25 25))
     ((1 1 1) (25 25 25 25)) ...))
|#
```

FIGURE 4.15 The function make-melody is responsible for creating a melody from the patterns thus far gathered.

```
(setf (get 's 'syntax) '(p e a))
(setf (get 'p 'syntax) '(s a c))
(setf (get 'e 'syntax) '(s p a c))
(setf (get 'a 'syntax) '(e c))
(setf (get 'c 'syntax) '(s p e a))

(setf (get 's 'meaning) '(0))
(setf (get 'p 'meaning) '(2 -2))
(setf (get 'e 'meaning) '(1 -1))
(setf (get 'a 'meaning) '(4 -4))
(setf (get 'c 'meaning) '(3 -3))
```

FIGURE 4.16 Property lists for the SPEAC system showing both their syntax and their actual meanings.

```
1.(defun generate-speac nil
2.  (get-speac (choose-one '(s p e a c))
3.              *rough-phrase-length*))
```

```
#|
 Calling (generate-speac)
 generate-speac returned (c a c a c ...)
 |#
```

a.

```
1.(defun get-speac (speac-character end-number)
2.  (if (zerop end-number)
3.      (list 'c)
4.      (cons speac-character
5.          (get-speac
6.            (choose-one (get speac-character 'syntax))
7.            (if (equal speac-character 'a)
8.                (1- end-number)
9.                end-number)))))
```

```
#|
 Calling (get-speac p 6)
  Calling (get-speac c 6)
   Calling (get-speac e 6)
    Calling (get-speac p 6)
     Calling (get-speac a 6)
      ...
    get-speac returned (a c s e p ...)
    get-speac returned (p a c s e ...)
   get-speac returned (e p a c s ...)
  get-speac returned (c e p a c ...)
 get-speac returned (p c e p a ...)
 |#
```

b.

```
1.(defun choose-one (objects)
2.  (nth (random (length objects) (make-random-state t))
3.      objects))
```

```
#|
 Calling (choose-one (2 3))
 choose-one returned 2
 Calling (choose-one (s p e a c))
 choose-one returned e
 |#
```

c.

FIGURE 4.17   The generate-speac sequence of functions.
a) The function generate-speac, found in line 3 of make-
melody (Figure 4.15). b) The function get-speac, found in
line 2 of generate-speac. c) The function choose-one,
found in line 6 of get-speac and elsewhere.

```
1.(defun find-it (meaning signatures)
2.   (cond ((null signatures)
3.          nil)
4.         ((funcall (function member)
5.                   (abs (first-of-first signatures))
6.                   (mapcar (function abs) meaning))
7.          (second-of-first signatures))
8.         (t
9.          (find-it meaning (rest signatures)))))

#|
 Calling (find-it
   (2 -2) ((-2 ((1 -3) (64 65 62)))
   (0 ((-1 1) (72 71 72)))
   (-2 ((1 -3) (71 72 69)))
   (0 ((-2 2) (79 77 79)))
   (2 ((-1 3) (77 76 79))) ...))
 find-it returned
   ((1 -3) (64 65 62))
|#
```

a.

FIGURE 4.18   The find-it sequence. a) The function find-it, found in line 2 of relate. b) The function relate, found in line 2 of associate. c) The function associate, found with generate-speac in line 3 of make-melody (Figure 4.15).

could also develop proportional strategies so that large intervals, for example, could vary depending on the local environment (i.e., a 4 is small in a work of mostly 7s but large in a work of mostly 2s).

The function relate (see Figure 4.18b) recursively matches its meanings argument with the directions (the first number in each sublist) of its signatures argument and returns a list of discovered matches. The function returns only the cdrs of the signatures that contain intervals and notes from the pattern-matching process. The use of let in relate ensures that if find-it finds no meaning, one will be found for it through the use of choose-one. Typically in large works, there should be no problem in finding a signature. It is also easy enough to change the lexicon of Figure 4.16 to use larger numbers for works with frequent leaps.

The function associate in Figure 4.18c relates its second argument to its first argument and returns the result, which contains both intervals and notes. We now have a melody that corresponds to the backbone created by get-speac (Figure 4.17b).

```
1.(defun relate (meanings signatures)
2.  (let ((find (find-it (first meanings) signatures)))
3.    (if (null meanings)
4.        nil
5.        (cons
6.          (if find
7.              find
8.              (second (choose-one signatures)))
9.          (relate (rest meanings) signatures)))))

#|
 Calling (relate
   ((1 -1) (0) (1 -1) (0) (1 -1) ...)
   ((-2 ((1 -3) (64 65 62)))
    (0 ((-1 1) (72 71 72)))
    (-2 ((1 -3) (71 72 69)))
    (0 ((-2 2) (79 77 79)))
    (2 ((-1 3) (77 76 79))) ...))
   ...
 relate returned
   (((-2 3) (71 69 72))
    ((-1 1) (72 71 72))
    ((-2 3) (71 69 72))
    ((-1 1) (72 71 72))
    ((-2 3) (71 69 72)) ...)
 |#
```

b.

```
1.(defun associate (generated-list signatures)
2.  (relate
3.    (mapcar
4.      (function (lambda (syntax) (get syntax 'meaning)))
5.      generated-list)
6.    signatures))

#|
 Calling (associate (a e a e a ...)
   ((-2 ((1 -3) (64 65 62)))
    (0 ((-1 1) (72 71 72)))
    (-2 ((1 -3) (71 72 69)))
    (0 ((-2 2) (79 77 79)))
    (2 ((-1 3) (77 76 79))) ...))
 associate returned
   (((-2 -2) (71 69 67))
    ((-2 3) (71 69 72))
    ((-2 -2) (71 69 67))
    ((-2 3) (71 69 72))
    ((-2 -2) (71 69 67)) ...)
 |#
```

c.

FIGURE 4.18   continued.

The function `create-rhythms`, invoked in Figure 4.15 and shown in Figure 4.19, receives as its first argument sets of patterns consisting of durations and the relationships of those durations, as discussed on pages 103–105 and shown in Figure 4.12b. Its second argument is the exact length of the melody already created in lines 2 through 10 in Figure 4.15. The purpose of this function is simply to group duration signatures into lists that ultimately match the length of the note list of the function running `create-rhythms`. Since those note lists are oblivious to beats at the current stage, `create-rhythms` provides whatever successful matches `pattern-match` provides (see lines 12 through 17 of `make-melody` in Figure 4.15).

Adding a Second Voice

In Figure 4.20, the function `add-second-voice` (called from line 7 of Figure 4.6) acts as a sub-sequence of the top level of the imitation sequence of `compose-invention` and creates an appropriate second voice for the nascent invention. First, it cleanses and arranges the current material to ready it for making a second voice. The function `imitate` then does the actual creation of a second line. How this works will be explained with Figure 4.22.

The function `align-beats`, in Figure 4.21a, processes its argument so that the result can be read as two lists of the new work consisting of parallel sub-lists arranged by beat. The first sub-list contains notes, and the second sub-list contains durations. Note in the sample run that the intervals and duration proportions have been removed since their job has been completed.

In Figure 4.21b, the function `make-beats`, used by `align-beats`, applies `collect-beats` to its two-list second argument, making beat-sized sub-lists of data. Since `collect-beats`, as will be seen, returns notes collected by beats, `make-beats` uses the number of collected notes (in line 8) to collect exactly the same number of durations to match them. This same number is used in lines 11 and 13 to `nthcdr` the second argument during recursion. The function `make-beats` is different from `get-beats` (Figure 4.10) in that the latter is exclusive to the `match` sequence of functions.

Figure 4.21c shows the function `collect-beats`, which uses its `number-of-beats` argument to gather beats from its second argument. The optional argument here defaults to 0 and allows addition of durations so that when they are equal to 100 the function quits recursing and returns the number of durations necessary to equal one beat.

```
1.(defun create-rhythms (patterns melody-length)
2.  (let ((trial-pattern (choose-one patterns)))
3.    (if (<= melody-length
4.            (length (second trial-pattern)))
5.        (list
6.          (list (first trial-pattern)
7.                (firstn melody-length
8.                        (second trial-pattern))))
9.        (cons trial-pattern
10.             (create-rhythms
11.               patterns
12.               (- melody-length
13.                  (length
                      (second trial-pattern)))))))))
```

```
#|
 Calling (create-rhythms
   (((1 1 1) (25 25 25 25))
    ((1 1 1) (25 25 25 25))
    ((1) (50 50))
    ((1) (50 50))
    ((1 1 1) (25 25 25 25)) ...) 54)
   ...
 create-rhythms returned
   (((1 1 1) (25 25 25 25))
    (nil (100))
    ((1 1 1) (25 25 25 25))
    ((1) (50 50))
    (nil (100)) ...)
|#
```

FIGURE 4.19 The function create-rhythms, found in line 12 of Figure 4.15, gets the material shown as a typical argument.

```
1.(defun add-second-voice nil
2.  (pair (layout (imitate meter (align-beats melody)))))
```

```
#|
 Calling (add-second-voice)
 add-second-voice returned
   (((64 65 62 72 71 ...) (25 25 25 25 25 ...))
    ((60 74 65 64 65 ...) (100 100 100 25 25 ...)))
|#
```

FIGURE 4.20 The function add-second-voice, the top level for the imitation sequence of the compose-invention program.

```
1.(defun align-beats (speac-melody)
2.   (let ((trial
3.           (make-beats
4.              1
5.            (list
6.              (apply 'append
7.                       (mapcar 'second
8.                                (first
9.                                 speac-melody)))
10.            (apply 'append
11.                     (mapcar 'second
12.                              (second
13.                               speac-melody)))))))
14.   (list (mapcar 'first trial) (mapcar 'second trial))))
```

```
#|
 Calling (align-beats
   ((((-1 -2) (77 76 74))
     ((-1 1) (72 71 72))
     ((-2 -2) (71 69 67))
     ((-2 3) (71 69 72))
     ((-1 1) (72 71 72)) ...)
    (((1 1 1) (25 25 25 25))
     ((1 1 1) (25 25 25 25))
     ((1 1 1) (25 25 25 25))
     ((1 1 1) (25 25 25 25))
     ((1 1 1) (25 25 25 25)) ...)))
 align-beats returned
  (((77 76 74 72)
    (71 72 71 69)
    (67 71 69 72)
    (72 71 72 71)
    (69 67 71 69) ...)
   ((25 25 25 25)
    (25 25 25 25)
    (25 25 25 25)
    (25 25 25 25)
    (25 25 25 25) ...))
|#
```

a.

FIGURE 4.21   a) The function `align-beats`, found in the second line of `add-second-voice` (Figure 4.20). b) The function `make-beats`, found in line 3 of `align-beats`. c) The function `collect-beats`, found in line 4 of `make-beats`.

```
1.(defun make-beats (number-of-beats music)
2.  (if (null (first music))
3.     nil
4.     (let ((trial (collect-beats number-of-beats
5.                                  music)))
6.       (cons
7.         (list trial
8.               (firstn (length trial) (second music)))
9.         (make-beats number-of-beats
10.                 (list
11.                   (nthcdr (length trial)
12.                             (first music))
13.                   (nthcdr (length trial)
14.                             (second music)))))))))
```

```
#|
 Calling (make-beats
  1
  ((64 65 62 71 69 ...) (25 25 25 25 25 ...)))
 Calling (make-beats
  1
  ((69 67 71 69 72 ...) (25 25 25 25 25 ...)))
 Calling (make-beats
   1
   ((72 71 69 67 71 ...) (25 25 25 25 25 ...)))
   ...
 make-beats returned
  (((72 71 69 67) (25 25 25 25))
   ((71 69 72 71) (25 25 25 25))
   ((69 67 71 69) (25 25 25 25))
   ((72 71 69 67) (25 25 25 25))
   ((71 69 72 71) (25 25 25 25)) ...)
 make-beats returned
  (((69 67 71 69) (25 25 25 25))
   ((72 71 69 67) (25 25 25 25))
   ((71 69 72 71) (25 25 25 25))
   ((69 67 71 69) (25 25 25 25))
   ((72 71 69 67) (25 25 25 25)) ...)
 make-beats returned
  (((64 65 62 71) (25 25 25 25))
   ((69 67 71 69) (25 25 25 25))
   ((72 71 69 67) (25 25 25 25))
   ((71 69 72 71) (25 25 25 25))
   ((69 67 71 69) (25 25 25 25)) ...)
|#
```

b.

FIGURE 4.21 continued.

```
1.(defun collect-beats (number-of-beats music
2.                            &optional (test 0))
3.   (cond ((null (first music))
4.          nil)
5.         ((>= test (* number-of-beats 100))
6.          nil)
7.         (t
8.           (cons (first-of-first music)
9.                 (collect-beats
10.                    number-of-beats
11.                    (list (rest (first music))
12.                          (rest (second music)))
13.                    (+ test
14.                       (first (second music))))))))))
```

```
#|
 Calling (collect-beats
   1
   ((71 69 72 72 71 ...) (25 25 25 25 25 ...)))
   Calling (collect-beats
     1
     ((69 72 72 71 72 ...) (25 25 25 25 25 ...)) 25)
     Calling (collect-beats
       1
       ((72 72 71 72 71 ...) (25 25 25 25 25 ...)) 50)
       Calling (collect-beats
         1
         ((72 71 72 71 69 ...) (25 25 25 25 25 ...)) 75)
         Calling (collect-beats
           1
           ((71 72 71 69 72 ...) (25 25 25 25 25 ...)) 100)
         collect-beats returned nil
       collect-beats returned (72)
     collect-beats returned (72 72)
   collect-beats returned (69 72 72)
 collect-beats returned (71 69 72 72)
|#
```

c.

FIGURE 4.21   continued.

Imitation

Like EMI, to be discussed in Chapter 5, the `compose-invention` program consists of a mix of inheritance and rules. The manner in which the `compose-invention` sequence creates melodies and rhythms is derived exclusively from the works called by the arguments to its top-level function. Thus it inherits materials (i.e., signatures) from its data. The functions designed to create imitation for these melodies differ in that they impose constraints on the music and are not derived in any way from the original works. These rules will help to make a more invention-like final output.

Figure 4.22 shows the five major functions designed to create imitation in the `compose-invention` program. The first, `imitate`, creates the imitative line for `compose-invention` as well as the countersubjects (the contrasting accompaniments to imitating lines) that will be injected into the originally composed melodic line. In line 2 of Figure 4.22a, a local variable `working-length` is twice the size of `meter` since `imitate` will successively `cdr` through its second argument by making bar-length countersubjects for both its upper and lower voices. This avoids problems during recursion since the function has to rock back and forth in invention style between its voices, creating countersubjects for each voice in turn. Lines 7 through 12 are the core of `imitate`. As will be seen in the description of `imitate-it`, the voices will alternatively erase and re-place meter-sized numbers of beats of first the second voice and then the first voice with quarter-note consonances (see bars 3 and 4 of Figure 5.1 for a musical example of this).

Figure 4.22b, `imitate-it`, provides the basic thrust for `imitate`. This function creates a countersubject for its second argument by beginning it in the second bar (according to `meter`) of the slowly evolving invention. Absolutely no attention is paid here to whether or not the new voices will fit with one another. This is inconsequential because one or the other of the voices will be replaced with consonant material according to `counter-it` in line 6 and `create-countersubject` in line 14.

The function `rest-beats`, shown in Figure 4.22c, makes rests. This is useful for openings of inventions, since the left hand of the performer usually rests while the right hand plays the subject (see Figure 4.4 for a musical example of this). Note that the variable `quarter-rest`, which was `setq`'ed in Figure 4.3, now becomes a convenient way to avoid having to present data in the function proper.

The function `create-countersubject`, shown in Figure 4.22d, is responsible for creating quarter-note countersubjects that are consonant with the emerging invention. It accomplishes this by `append`'ing a `meter`-length set of note lists from different parts of the two lines it is given (see

```
1.(defun imitate (meter beated-voice)
2.  (let ((working-length (* meter 2)))
3.    (if (null
4.           (nthcdr working-length (first beated-voice)))
5.        nil
6.        (append
7.          (imitate-it meter
8.                      (list
9.                        (firstn working-length
10.                          (first beated-voice))
11.                        (firstn working-length
12.                          (second beated-voice))))
13.          (imitate meter
14.                   (list
15.                     (nthcdr working-length
16.                       (first beated-voice))
17.                     (nthcdr working-length
18.                       (second beated-voice)))))))))))
```

```
#|
  Calling (imitate
    2
    (((71 69 67 77)
      (76 74 64 65)
      (62 71 69 67)
      (71 69 72 72)
      (71 72 71 69) ...)
     ((25 25 25 25)
      (25 25 25 25)
      (25 25 25 25)
      (25 25 25 25)
      (25 25 25 25) ...)))
   ...
```

a.

FIGURE 4.22   The `imitate` sequence of functions. a) The function `imitate`, found in the second line of `add-second-voice` (Figure 4.20). b) The function `imitate-it`, found in line 7 of `imitate`, with a sample run. c) The function `rest-beats`, found in line 12 of `imitate-it`. d) The function `create-countersubject`, found in line 14 of `imitate-it`. e) The function `counter-it`, found in line 6 of `create-countersubject`.

```
  imitate returned
   ((((71 69 67 77) (76 74 64 65) (67) (72))
     ((25 25 25 25) (25 25 25 25) (100) (100)))
    (((67) (72) (71 69 67 77) (76 74 64 65))
     ((100) (100) (25 25 25 25) (25 25 25 25)))
    (((71 72 71 69) (72 72 71 72) (74) (76))
     ((25 25 25 25) (25 25 25 25) (100) (100)))
    (((74) (76) (71 72 71 69) (72 72 71 72))
     ((100) (100) (25 25 25 25) (25 25 25 25)))
    (((72 72 71 72) (71 69 72 72) (76) (74))
     ((25 25 25 25) (25 25 25 25) (100) (100))) ...)
  |#
```

a. continued.

```
1.(defun imitate-it (meter beated-voice)
2.   (let ((new-work
3.      (list beated-voice
4.            (list
5.              (append
6.                (counter-it meter
7.                            (firstn meter
8.                             (first beated-voice)))
9.               (firstn meter (first beated-voice)))
10.             (append
11.              (mapcar 'second
12.                      (second (rest-beats meter)))
13.               (firstn meter (second beated-voice)))))))
14.   (list (create-countersubject meter new-work)
15.         (second new-work))))
```

```
#|
 Calling (imitate-it
   2
   (((64 65 62 77)
     (76 74 71 69)
     (72 71 69 67)
     (71 69 72 71))
    ((25 25 25 25)
     (25 25 25 25)
     (25 25 25 25)
     (25 25 25 25))))
 imitate-it returned
   ((((64 65 62 77) (76 74 71 69) (60) (72))
     ((25 25 25 25) (25 25 25 25) (100) (100)))
    (((60) (72) (64 65 62 77) (76 74 71 69))
     ((100) (100) (25 25 25 25) (25 25 25 25))))
  |#
```

b.

FIGURE 4.22 continued.

```
1.(defun rest-beats (meter)
2.  (list
3.    (make-list meter
4.                :initial-element
5.                  (first quarter-rest))
6.    (make-list meter
7.                :initial-element
8.                  (second quarter-rest))))

#|
 Calling (rest-beats 3)
 rest-beats returned
  (((nil (0)) (nil (0)) (nil (0)))
    ((nil (100)) (nil (100)) (nil (100))))
|#
```

c.

```
1.(defun create-countersubject (meter two-lines-of-music)
2.  (list
3.    (append (firstn meter
4.                    (first-of-first
5.                      two-lines-of-music))
6.            (counter-it meter
7.                        (nthcdr meter
8.                                (first (second
9.                                  two-lines-of-music)))))
10.   (append (firstn meter
11.                   (second-of-first
12.                     two-lines-of-music))
13.           (make-list
14.             meter
15.             :initial-element
16.               (second (second quarter-rest)))))))

#|
 Calling (create-countersubject
   2
   ((((72 71 72 64)
      (65 62 72 71)
      (72 64 65 62)
      (72 71 72 64))
     ((25 25 25 25)
      (25 25 25 25)
      (25 25 25 25)
      (25 25 25 25)))
    (((69) (62) (72 71 72 64) (65 62 72 71))
     ((100) (100) (25 25 25 25) (25 25 25 25)))))
 create-countersubject returned
  (((72 71 72 64) (65 62 72 71) (69) (62))
    ((25 25 25 25) (25 25 25 25) (100) (100)))
|#
```

d.

FIGURE 4.22 continued.

```
1.(defun counter-it (meter beated-melody)
2.  (if (zerop meter)
3.      nil
4.      (cons
5.        (list
6.          (find-closest-consonance
7.            (first-of-first beated-melody)))
8.          (counter-it (1- meter) (rest beated-melody)))))))
```

```
#|
 Calling (counter-it 3 ((72 71) (72 71) (69 72)))
  Calling (counter-it 2 ((72 71) (69 72)))
   Calling (counter-it 1 ((69 72)))
    Calling (counter-it 0 nil)
    counter-it returned nil
   counter-it returned ((72))
  counter-it returned ((76) (72))
 counter-it returned ((76) (76) (72))
|#
```

e.

FIGURE 4.22   continued.

the use of first-of-first in line 4 and the parallel use of second-of-first in line 11). Again, access to quarter-rest is helpful in abstracting data (see line 16).

The function counter-it, shown in Figure 4.22e, finds a proper consonant note for the downbeat notes of the original melody. It provides as many of these as its first argument requires. These consonant notes are then given the previously mentioned durations (in lines 10–12 of create-countersubject).

Figure 4.23 shows two functions that ensure downbeats are consonant. The first, find-closest-consonance, shown in Figure 4.23a, operates find-closest on (1) a pitch either a third up or down from the note being tested (i.e., 4 in Figure 4.23a); (2) the note itself; and (3) the major-scale that was setq'ed in Figure 4.3. The random nature of the first argument to find-closest allows for interesting variations in the music, and the second argument ensures that leaps are not too extensive.

In Figure 4.23b, the support function find-closest is shown. Lines 2 and 3 stop the function if its third argument is null (it is a good idea to avoid the possibility of endless recursion, although the function should be given the right arguments in the first place). Line 4 tests for whether the second number is equal to or greater than the note being tested. If this is true, then the code further tests (lines 6–10) for whether the

```
1.(defun find-closest-consonance (note)
2.  (find-closest (funcall (choose-one '(+ -)) note 4)
3.                note
4.                major-scale))
```

```
#|
 Calling (find-closest-consonance 71)
 find-closest-consonance returned 74
 Calling (find-closest-consonance 76)
 find-closest-consonance returned 79
|#
```

                a.

```
1.(defun find-closest (note other-note right-note-list)
2.  (cond ((null (rest right-note-list))
3.         (first right-note-list))
4.        ((>= (second right-note-list) note)
5.         (if (and
6.              (not (equal (- other-note
7.                             (first right-note-list))
8.                          5))
9.              (<= (- note (first right-note-list))
10.                 (- (second right-note-list) note)))
11.            (first right-note-list)
12.            (second right-note-list)))
13.       (t
14.         (find-closest note
15.                       other-note
16.                       (rest right-note-list))))))
```

```
#|
 Calling (find-closest 67 71 (36 38 40 41 43 ...))
  Calling (find-closest 67 71 (38 40 41 43 45 ...))
    ...
  find-closest returned 67
 find-closest returned 67
|#
```

                b.

FIGURE 4.23 The consonance sequence of functions. a) The function find-closest-consonance, found in line 6 of counter-it (Figure 4.22e). b) The function find-closest, found in line 2 of find-closest-consonance.

potentially right note is a fourth or second (dissonance in this style) of the original note (second argument in the figure). If this condition is not true, then the first note in the third argument is chosen (see line 11). If the condition is true, the second note in the third argument is returned (see line 12). These lines of code (4 through 12 of `find-closest`) may be challenging to readers who know either LISP or music well but not both. Readers are encouraged to work through this code carefully with fragments of code and music paper to see (and hear) the results of the tests involved here. The complexity may be trying, but junctures such as this are key elements in understanding how programming musical problems such as consonance can occasionally create code that is difficult to decipher.

The function `layout`, shown in Figure 4.24, receives pattern-matched lists of the melodic and durational sequences of the `compose-invention` program and lays out the data as lists of notes and durations. The `apply-append` trick discussed in Chapter 3 occurs here in lines 6 and 8 and ensures that sub-lists, created for pattern matching, are removed. Because the processes of creating the melodies and rhythms are parallel, both are returned in exactly the same ways.

Figure 4.25 shows the function `pair`, which is used to line up the sub-lists of its argument in proper rows of pitches and durations. This function makes calls to `mapcar` for each of the four note and duration lists. It then uses the `apply-append` trick to merge the sub-lists into continuous numbers. The output is simply two lists of two sub-lists, each containing note and duration numbers respectively.

Figure 4.26 shows the function `every-other`, which collects every other member of its single list argument. This function is used by `pair` twice (see lines 3 and 4 in Figure 4.25), in the manner shown in the sample run in Figure 4.26. All of the data that was realigned during the `imitate` sequence is put here into more normal order.

Cadence

The `cadence` sequence of functions is shown in Figure 4.27. The function `cadence-it` (Figure 4.27a) is found in line 8 of `compose-invention` in Figure 4.6. It operates `insert-cadence` (Figure 4.27b), giving it the current state of the work with a transposed version of its second voice. The function `insert-cadence` breaks its argument into beats and feeds it to `make-a-cadence` (Figure 4.27c), which produces lists that need rectifying through a double use of `mapcar` in order to read out correctly. Note the use of the program variable `*minimum-length*` in Figure 4.27b (line 3). It is passed to `make-a-cadence`, which reduces it incrementally as beats of the work are collected.

```
1.(defun layout (imitate-lists)
2.  (if (null imitate-lists)
3.      nil
4.      (cons
5.        (list
6.          (apply 'append
7.                 (first (first imitate-lists)))
8.          (apply 'append
9.                 (second (first imitate-lists))))
10.        (layout (rest imitate-lists)))))
```

```
#|
 Calling (layout
  (((((64 65 62 77) (76 74 72 71) (60) (72))
    ((25 25 25 25) (25 25 25 25) (100) (100)))
   (((67) (72) (64 65 62 77) (76 74 72 71))
    ((100) (100) (25 25 25 25) (25 25 25 25))))

   (((71 72 71 69) (67 71 69 72) (74) (71))
    ((25 25 25 25) (25 25 25 25) (100) (100)))
   (((67) (64) (71 72 71 69) (67 71 69 72))
    ((100) (100) (25 25 25 25) (25 25 25 25))))
   (((72 72 71 72) (71 69 67 71) (69) (67))
    ((25 25 25 25) (25 25 25 25) (100) (100))) ...))
   ...
 layout returned
  (((64 65 62 77 76 ...) (25 25 25 25 25 ...))
   ((67 72 64 65 62 ...) (100 100 25 25 25 ...))
   ((71 72 71 69 67 ...) (25 25 25 25 25 ...))
   ((67 64 71 72 71 ...) (100 100 25 25 25 ...))
   ((72 72 71 72 71 ...) (25 25 25 25 25 ...)) ...)
|#
```

FIGURE 4.24 The function layout, found in line 2 of add-second-voice (Figure 4.20).

The actual value of *minimum-length* will not be altered by this process, however; only the value of the temporary variable of minimum-length in make-a-cadence will be affected.

The idea in make-a-cadence is not to let the music cadence too early (hence the use of *minimum-length* in insert-cadence). After zero has been reached, the function continues to search for notes belonging to dominant, at which time it adds a final tonic. Note that if it doesn't find notes belonging to dominant, or if its first argument is higher than the length of the second argument's number of lists, then no cadence will occur in the output.

Lines 11 through 26 of make-a-cadence are the analysis portion of the code. The first-note and second-note variables (set earlier in

```
1.(defun pair (work-lists)
2.  (let ((paired-voice-lists
3.            (list (every-other work-lists)
4.                  (every-other (rest work-lists)))))
5.    (list
6.      (list
7.        (apply 'append
8.                (mapcar 'first
9.                         (first
10.                         paired-voice-lists)))
11.       (apply 'append
12.                (mapcar 'second
13.                         (first
14.                         paired-voice-lists))))
15.   (list
16.       (apply 'append
17.                (mapcar 'first
18.                         (second
19.                         paired-voice-lists)))
20.       (apply 'append
21.                (mapcar 'second
22.                         (second
23.                         paired-voice-lists)))))))))

#|
Calling (pair
  (((72 71 72 71 69 ...) (25 25 25 25 25 ...))
   ((69 65 77 72 71 ...) (100 100 100 25 25 ...))
   ((69 67 77 76 74 ...) (50 50 50 50 50 ...))
   ((65 74 71 69 67 ...) (100 100 100 50 50 ...))
   ((69 67 77 76 74 ...) (50 50 50 50 50 ...)) ...))
 pair returned
  (((72 71 72 71 69 ...) (25 25 25 25 25 ...))
   ((69 65 77 72 71 ...) (100 100 100 25 25 ...)))
|#
```

FIGURE 4.25 The function pair, found in line 2 of add-second-voice (Figure 4.20).

lines 5 through 10) are the downbeat portion of the current beat, and member (lines 14 and 15) returns non-nil only when the notes at this point belong to the dominant chord projected in all octaves. Lines 20 and 25 of make-a-cadence demonstrate why it was necessary to have both a tonic and a tonic-note setq in Figure 4.3. The tonic represents the notes of a tonic chord in all octaves and is used here for the upper voice, which may, at least for this program, end on any member of the chord. The tonic-note represents only the pitch-class of tonic notes

```
1.(defun every-other (objects)
2.  (if (null objects)
3.       nil
4.       (cons (first objects)
5.              (every-other (nthcdr 2 objects)))))
```

```
#|
 Calling (every-other
  (((77 76 74 64 74 ...) (50 50 50 50 100 ...))
   ((81 77 77 76 74 ...) (100 100 50 50 50 ...))
   ((67 77 76 74 71 ...) (50 50 50 50 100 ...))
   ((64 72 67 77 76 ...) (100 100 50 50 50 ...))
   ((69 72 72 71 65 ...) (50 50 50 50 100 ...)) ...))
   ...
 every-other returned
  (((77 76 74 64 74 ...) (50 50 50 50 100 ...))
   ((67 77 76 74 71 ...) (50 50 50 50 100 ...))
   ((69 72 72 71 65 ...) (50 50 50 50 100 ...))
   ((72 71 72 71 76 ...) (50 50 50 50 100 ...))
   ((72 71 69 72 69 ...) (50 50 50 50 100 ...)) ...)
|#
```

FIGURE 4.26 The function `every-other`, along with a sample run. It appears in lines 3 and 4 of `pair` (Figure 4.25).

and ensures that the final cadence will have a tonic note in the bass and hence produce a tonic chord in root position.

In Figure 4.28, the function `transpose-second-voice` projects the newly created imitative line down one octave so that it will not become confused with the first voice. It does this by mapping a no-name function that subtracts 12 from the pitch numbers of the second line. Neither the first line nor the durations of the second line are affected by this process. Rests are introduced by the use of `make-list` in line 4 with its `initial-element` set to 0.

Miscellaneous Functions

The function `firstn`, shown in Figure 4.29a and used in many of the functions in the previous figures, returns the `nth` amount of its list argument. This function operates like `nthcdr` except that it binds the `cars` of the list it is provided into a new list `number` long. Figures 4.29b and 4.29c are both straightforward utilities that make the code more readable. These are synonyms for `caar` and `cadar`.

```
1.(defun cadence-it nil
2.  (insert-cadence
3     (transpose-second-voice meter
4.                            initial-new-composition)))
```

```
#|
 Calling (cadence-it)
 cadence-it returned
  ((((71 69 67 77) (25 25 25 25))
    ((76 74 64 65) (25 25 25 25))
    ((62 71 69 67) (25 25 25 25))
    ((74) (100)) ((72) (100)) ...)
   (((0) (100)) ((0) (100)) ((0) (100))
    ((59 57 55 65) (25 25 25 25))
    ((64 62 52 53) (25 25 25 25)) ...))
|#
```

a.

```
1.(defun insert-cadence (work)
2.  (let ((cadenced-work
3.    (make-a-cadence *minimum-length*
4.                    (mapcar
5.                     (function (lambda (x)
6.                                (make-beats 1 x)))
7.                     work))))
8.    (list (mapcar 'first cadenced-work)
9.          (mapcar 'second cadenced-work))))
```

```
#|
  Calling (insert-cadence
   (((71 69 67 77 76 ...) (25 25 25 25 25 ...))
    ((0 0 0 59 57 ...) (100 100 100 25 25 ...)))))
  insert-cadence returned
   (((((71 69 67 77) (25 25 25 25))
     ((76 74 64 65) (25 25 25 25))
     ((62 71 69 67) (25 25 25 25))
     ((74) (100)) ((72) (100)) ...)
    (((0) (100)) ((0) (100)) ((0) (100))
     ((59 57 55 65) (25 25 25 25))
     ((64 62 52 53) (25 25 25 25)) ...))
|#
```

b.

FIGURE 4.27 The cadence sequence of functions. a) The function cadence-it, found in line 8 of compose-invention (Figure 4.6). b) The function insert-cadence, found in line 2 of cadence-it. c) The function make-a-cadence, found in line 3 of insert-cadence.

```
1.(defun make-a-cadence (minimum-length beated-work)
2.  (let ((beat
3.          (list (first-of-first beated-work)
4.                (first (second beated-work))))
5.         (first-note
6.           (first-of-first
7.             (first-of-first beated-work)))
8.         (second-note
9.           (first-of-first
10.            (first (second beated-work)))))
11.   (cond ((null (first beated-work))
12.          nil)
13.         ((and (<= minimum-length 0)
14.               (member first-note dominant)
15.               (member second-note dominant))
16.          (list beat
17.                (nest 2
18.                      (find-closest first-note
19.                                    first-note
20.                                    tonic)
21.                (list qtr)
22.                (list
23.                   (find-closest second-note
24.                                 second-note
25.                                 tonic-note))
26.                (list qtr))))
27.         (t
28.           (cons
29.             beat
30.             (make-a-cadence (1- minimum-length)
31.                             (list
32.                               (rest
33.                                 (first
34.                                   beated-work))
35.                               (rest
36.                                 (second
37.                                   beated-work)))))))))
```

c.

FIGURE 4.27   continued.

```
#|
  Calling (make-a-cadence
    5
    ((((71 69 67 77) (25 25 25 25))
      ((76 74 64 65) (25 25 25 25))
      ((62 71 69 67) (25 25 25 25))
      ((74) (100)) ((72) (100)) ...)
     (((0) (100))
      ((0) (100))
      ((0) (100))
      ((59 57 55 65) (25 25 25 25))
      ((64 62 52 53) (25 25 25 25)) ...)))
    ...
  make-a-cadence returned
   ((((71 69 67 77) (25 25 25 25)) ((0) (100)))
    (((76 74 64 65) (25 25 25 25)) ((0) (100)))
    (((62 71 69 67) (25 25 25 25)) ((0) (100)))
    (((74) (100)) ((59 57 55 65) (25 25 25 25)))
    (((72) (100)) ((64 62 52 53) (25 25 25 25))) ...)
|#
```

c. continued.

FIGURE 4.27   continued.

Figure 4.30 presents the functions nest and nest-list, which hide rather ugly sub-listings (successive calls to the function list). This is necessary in make-a-cadence due to the delicate and complex form of the data at the point these two functions are used in the program. The first function, nest (Figure 4.30a), has two arguments. The first, number-of-nestings, represents the number of calls to nest-list (see line 2 of Figure 4.30b) required by the call. Since this will vary by circumstance, the use of &rest allows for a variable number of objects to be sub-listed (the number of second arguments must be at least twice the first argument). The separate function nest-list is required here so that &rest will not treat a recursive call to nest (were it one function) as a single listed object that would force an error. Note that the objects may be atoms or lists of any type: The data is not changed here except for being sub-listed.

The function get-length, shown in Figure 4.31 and used in line 17 of Figure 4.15, ensures that the returned sequence of durations matches in length the list of pitches that create-rhythms receives. It accomplishes this by adding the second elements of successive calls to its argument.

```
1.(defun transpose-second-voice (meter work)
2.   (list (first work)
3.          (list
4.            (append (make-list meter
5.                              :initial-element 0)
6.                  (nthcdr meter
7.                      (mapcar
8.                        (function
9.                          (lambda (x) (- x 12)))
10.                        (first (second work)))))
11.          (second (second work)))))))

#|
 Calling (transpose-second-voice
   3
   (((64 65 62 77 76 ...) (25 25 25 25 25 ...))
    ((60 72 76 64 65 ...) (100 100 100 25 25 ...)))))
 transpose-second-voice returned
   (((64 65 62 77 76 ...) (25 25 25 25 25 ...))
    ((0 0 0 52 53 ...) (100 100 100 25 25 ...))))
|#
```

FIGURE 4.28   The function `transpose-second-voice`.

SAMPLE INVENTIONS

Figure 4.32 shows the output of two runs of `compose-invention`. It should be noted that they were composed by the machine without editing or aesthetic selection. Obviously, culling the best from a fair amount of composition could produce much more interesting results. For the true inheritance of Bach's style to take place, a much more elaborate program would be necessary. This more elaborate program is presented in the description of EMI in the next chapter.

Signatures from both inventions of Figure 4.4 and Figure 4.5 can be found in Figure 4.32. Both of the works in the database contain a figure consisting of a half step down and a return up (see the last three eighth notes of bar 1 of Invention No. 1 and the first three sixteenth notes of Invention No. 5). More extensive pattern matching produces a similar opening, as shown in the full-length Bach invention imitation (see Figure 5.1), for which two complete inventions were used as the database. The minor sevenths that occur in bar 3, right hand, and bar 4, left hand, of Figure 4.32a are part of a signature based on an apparent match between bar 5 of Invention No. 1 (beats 1 to 2) and bar 6 of Invention No. 5 (beat 3).

```
1.(defun firstn (number objects)
2.  (butlast objects (- (length objects) number)))
```

```
#|
 Calling (firstn 3 (0 60 62 64 65 ...))
 firstn returned (0 60 62)
|#
```

a.

```
1.(defun first-of-first (list) (caar list))
```

```
#|
 Calling (first-of-first
  (((60 -1) (0 60 59))
   ((2 2) (60 62 64))
   ((-65 62) (65 0 62))
   ((2 2) (60 62 64))
   ((2 -3) (65 67 64)) ...))
 first-of-first returned (60 -1)
|#
1.(defun second-of-first (list) (cadar list))
```

```
#|
 Calling (second-of-first
  ((-2 ((1 -3) (64 65 62)))
   (0 ((-1 1) (72 71 72)))
   (-2 ((1 -3) (71 72 69)))
   (0 ((-2 2) (79 77 79)))
   (2 ((-1 3) (77 76 79))) ...))
 second-of-first returned ((1 -3) (64 65 62))
|#
```

b.

FIGURE 4.29 a) The function `firstn` and a sample run. b) The functions `first-of-first` and `second-of-first`.

The program `compose-invention` is a small program designed to introduce readers to programming, musical potentials of programming in LISP, linguistic possibilities for generating phrases, and pattern matching as a component of style recognition. For possibly better results in using this program, one might try: (1) building larger note and duration lists; (2) spending a lot of time fine-tuning the variables, even creating new ones; and (3) building other components. One might also branch into the works and styles of other composers using the same basic techniques presented here. With skills learned from Chapters 3 and 4, along with a good LISP

```
1.(defun nest (number-of-nestings &rest objects)
2.  (nest-list number-of-nestings objects))
```

```
#|
 Calling (nest 2 72 (100) (60) (100))
 nest returned (((72) (100)) ((60) (100)))
 |#
```

a.

```
1.(defun nest-list (number-of-nestings objects)
2. (if (eq number-of-nestings 1)(list objects)
3.     (cons (list (first objects))
4.               (second objects))
5..         (nest-list (1- number-of-nestings)
6.                       (nthcdr 2 objects)))))
```

```
#|
 Calling (nest-list 2 (72 (100) (60) (100)))
  Calling (nest-list 1 ((60) (100)))
  nest-list returned (((60) (100)))
 nest-list returned (((72) (100)) ((60) (100)))
 |#
```

b.

FIGURE 4.30   a) The function nest. b) The function nest-list.

```
1.(defun get-length (melody-list)
2.  (if (null melody-list)
3.      0
4.      (+ (if (not (null melody-list))
5.             (length (second-of-first melody-list))
6.             0)
7.         (get-length (rest melody-list))))))
```

```
#|
 Calling (get-length
  (((-1 1) (72 71 72))
   ((-2 -2) (71 69 67))
   ((-1 -2) (77 76 74))
   ((-2 -2) (71 69 67))
   ((-1 -2) (77 76 74)) ...))
  ...
 get-length returned 39
 |#
```

FIGURE 4.31   The function get-length.

FIGURE 4.32 Two runs of `compose-invention` in musical notation.

text (see bibliography to Chapter 3), one should be able to accomplish interesting variations of the code presented here for application to a diversity of musical situations.

Thus, by using principles discussed in Chapters 2 and 3, along with basic pattern-matching techniques, a composing program has been created using LISP. While simple, the results are interesting and, being loaded with signatures, similar to the music in the databases. Using these techniques and expanding them to include harmony and ATN, I have built extensive systems for the study and replication of musical style. Further examples are given in the next chapter.

BIBLIOGRAPHY

Baroni, Mario, and Laura Callegari, eds. *Musical Grammars and Computer Analysis: Atti del Convegno (Modena, 4–6 Ottobre 1982)*. Florence, Italy: L. S. Olschki, 1984.

Fu, K. S. *Syntactic Pattern Recognition and Applications*. Englewood Cliffs, N.J.: Prentice-Hall, 1982.

Meehan, James R. "An Artificial Intelligence Approach to Tonal Music Theory." *Computer Music Journal* 4,2 (Summer 1980): 60–65.

MUSICAL EXAMPLES

. . . .

INTRODUCTION

This chapter first presents two short Bach-like inventions composed by the program EMI. These works set the stage for a short but in-depth discussion of the EMI program. The rest of the chapter presents scores and discussions of several full movements, along with sections of other movements. Others are given in Cope (1991). A wide variety of styles are presented here. One common theme throughout this chapter and the next is that of identifying signatures in the original compositions that recur in the works created by EMI.

BACH INVENTIONS

Two machine-composed imitations of Bach inventions were completed about four months apart (July 18 and November 27, 1988) at the EMI studio. Bach's inventions were entered as lists of notes and durations without ornamentation, which was appropriately restored by hand after machine composition took place. Rules for the form, that is, a two-voice work with staggered and imitative entrances, were written in special code not necessary for non-contrapuntal works (for further information on this, see "Counterpoint" later in this chapter). It should be noted that the inventions that follow were composed by more elaborate code than the `compose-invention` program articulated in Chapter 4.

FIGURE 5.1 EMI's *Invention 1*; the initial motive was based on opening motives of Bach's Invention No. 2 and Invention No. 5

FIGURE 5.1 continued.

However, it is not hard to imagine the relatively small amount of added code it would take for `compose-invention` to create the refinements presented in the more elegant inventions created by EMI.

The first EMI invention was based on two Bach inventions (No. 2 and No. 5) with some signatures derived from other works by Bach. The initial motive of *Invention 1* by EMI (shown in Figure 5.1) was clearly derived from an overlay of the opening motives of the two Bach inventions (see Figures 5.2 and 5.3). Rhythm aside, the themes of both of these inventions are intervallically almost identical. The program simply continued the scale begun by what it perceived to be a signature of the composer (appearing as it did as principal motive in both works). The opening durations of EMI's invention seem to be a mean of the two Bach openings.

Since the rules in the program coerce skipping in one voice when stepping in the other and vice versa, the triadic leaps in the right hand during the second entrance of the theme seem logical. The high number of contrary motions also is a result of rules built into the program. Interestingly, these include forced opposite direction that creates the triadic inversion in bar 3 (i.e., bar 2 right hand is inverted in bar 3 left hand). The use of sequence (bars 1 and 3 of the right hand) follows from similar

FIGURE 5.2   The opening of Bach's Invention No. 2 (ornamentation has been omitted).

compositional rules, but the origins of the left hand in bar 4 are not clear. From this point on, what is signature and what is machine composition (discussed in the next section on EMI) is not known. The form derived from the actual inventions being used provided little more than a simple two-voice structure with staggered entrances. The quasi-stretto in bar 20, for example, was suggested by the derived form.

One thing that jumps out is that the final cadence was derived from signatures in other works (e.g., the Bourrée of Bach's Ouverture in F Major, which ends in this exact manner). These works were utilized because of the few signatures that were found in the two inventions and the concomitant desire to discover Bach's *keyboard* style as it relates to his inventions.

FIGURE 5.3   The opening of Bach's Invention No. 5.

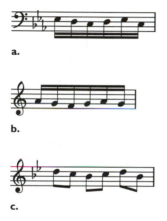

a.

b.

c.

FIGURE 5.4   a) Bach's Invention No. 5, bar 31.
b) Bach's Invention No. 2, bar 14.
c) EMI *Invention 1,* bar 5.

Another interesting figure, in the right hand of bar 3 of the new composition, appears throughout Bach's Invention No. 5 but rarely in Invention
No. 2. However, a close look reveals that a variant of it appears often
enough in Invention No. 2 to create a pattern match, so the EMI program
recognizes it as a signature and uses the Invention No. 5 figure almost
excessively in its own composition. Figure 5.4 shows examples from Bach's
inventions and then EMI's version. The rhythmic differences are arbitrary.

The EMI version could have easily read sixteenth notes as eighth notes since durations are relative.

The frequent use of leaps of a sixth and back again represent a good-example of how the program works. Analysis of both of Bach's inventions reveals that this motive occurs rarely in Invention No. 2 (see the right hand motion in measure 7 in Figure 5.2) and literally never in Invention No. 5. However, since the C or tonic should have been used instead of the left-hand G in measure 16 of Figure 5.1, for example (because it works harmonically and represents a closer solution), the motive *must* be a derived signature. The solution to this conundrum is in the windowing approach to pattern matching used in EMI's programs. Looking more closely at Invention No. 5 shows that every leap of a sixth does have an occurrence of a sixth in the opposite direction eventually, but only after intervening notes. This is disguised by the foreground detail but discovered by the flexible approach to motive discovery of the pattern-matching program.

Thus the brief (one-minute duration) EMI invention represents a grafting of signatures onto a form created by a two-voice, rules-based, voice-leading program (see next section). The result is stylistically believable and interesting if not entirely successful music.

EMI *Invention 2* (shown in Figure 5.5) is more difficult to analyze for signatures since the number of works utilized for its composition was large, having been derived from the entire set of fifteen Bach inventions. The opening theme appears to be a composite of signatures gathered from Inventions No. 8, No. 10, and No. 13 (see Figure 5.6). The right-hand accompaniment to the left-hand statement of the theme in bar 2, just like EMI's first invention, is a simple triadic outline and suggests no signature relationship. On the other hand, the four-note motive found in the right hand in the second half of measure 1 is a convincing signature found particularly in Bach Inventions No. 6, No. 7, and No. 9 (see Figure 5.7), although in the latter case the rhythm is not the same. It also appears in Invention No. 15 but with the leap interval of varying sizes and directions as shown in Figure 5.8.

The signature beginning in the right hand of bar 10 in EMI *Invention 2* can be found in Bach's Inventions No. 12 and No. 13 (see Figure 5.9). The left-hand figure starting in the second half of bar 18 can be found in several of Bach's inventions, particularly No. 6 and No. 15 (see Figure 5.10). The most common invention ending for Bach is the unison or octave. But he does end both Inventions No. 1 and No. 8 with chords, and the program used these as a signature in this particular work.

There are, of course, many other signatures present here that space does not permit showing. The interested reader is invited to make further comparisons to the originals.

EMI

The functions presented in Chapter 4 did not create the EMI inventions shown at the beginning of this chapter. They did, however, present enough of the theory and principles for readers to extend the code and compose similar works. The music that follows requires a more substantial leap of faith. The functions responsible for its creation are far too elaborate and lengthy to present here in their entirety. However, I can enumerate the various principles covered by that code and, at least to some extent, describe its operation in detail.

Texture in EMI has been calculated with various procedures. One of these follows a mapping process that calculates the number of pitch components on each beat in one or more of the compositions used as databases. This is accomplished on a phrase-by-phrase basis. If two works are being used for analysis, the program will randomly choose from analyzed phrases of one or the other of the works. Figure 5.11 represents the texture of the first phrase of Mozart's Sonata in B♭ Major, K. 333. The figure shows the number of notes occurring on each quarter-note beat. To match this map during the compositional process, the program doubles one or more of the voices (if the texture is more than three voices) or removes notes (if less). Seventh chords, missing a member when composed in three voices, can be reconstructed (without doubling) according to straightforward rules involving the presence of tension (dissonance).

Harmony, thus far expressed only in terms of consonance, tonic, and dominant, is a direct result of matching implied harmony (from generated melodies) to a complete lexicon of harmonic functions. This follows the traditional functional representations of classical Western European music. As with SPEAC, the representations are given meanings (i.e., tonic = C E G in all octaves) once the protocols (i.e., `(setf 'dom-inant '(tonic submediant))`) have been established in lists of function representations.

Cadences pose a particular set of problems similar to those encountered in the function `insert-cadence` in Figure 4.27 in combination with the c of the SPEAC system (see Figure 4.16). In fact, entire chord progressions themselves evolve from a series of SPEAC symbols that slowly reveal musical functions in parallel with melodic implications. While this may appear opaque in the abstract, one need only review the topic of SPEAC presented in Chapter 2 to see how it could be obtained.

Form is possibly the most difficult aspect of musical style to perceive and generate. In early editions of EMI, form was considered so difficult to program that I defined it explicitly without any computer control. It was accomplished through a set of symbols traditional to form texts such as A

FIGURE 5.5   *Invention 2* by EMI.

FIGURE 5.5 continued.

FIGURE 5.5   continued.

FIGURE 5.6   The first bar of Bach Inventions No. 8 (a),
No. 10 (b), and No, 13 (c).

FIGURE 5.7   From a) Bach's Invention No. 6 (bar 4),
b) Invention No. 7 (bar 22), c) Invention No. 9 (bar 17).

FIGURE 5.8   From Bach's Invention No. 15.
a) Bar 1. b) Bar 21. c) Bar 4. d) Bar 11.

FIGURE 5.9   a) Bach's Invention No. 12 (bar 18).
b) No. 13 (bar 23).

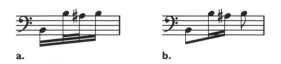

FIGURE 5.10   a) Bach's Invention No. 6 (bar 18).
b) No. 15 (bar 21).

I 1 2 2 2 I 1 2 2 2 I 1 2 2 2 I 2 3 1 2 I 2 2 2 2 I 3 1 1 1 I 2 2 2 2 I 3 1 1 1 I 3 3 3 3 I 2 2 1

FIGURE 5.11 A texture map of the first phrase of Mozart's Piano Sonata in B♭ Major, K. 333.

A′ B B′, where A refers to a theme and A′ (known as A "prime") to a variation, and where B refers to a contrast (here with its own prime) to A. Each letter represents a phrase of music. More recent forms of EMI include a music-encoding process that by its very nature (determining phrases by labeling cadence points) allows EMI to produce a rough analytic equivalent to the previous user input.

The EMI algorithm, shown in Figure 5.12, consists of six major steps. First, music must be coded as shown in Chapter 4. A minimum of two works of a single type must be coded as notes and durations before EMI can emulate a particular style. The more compositions present, the more convincingly the program imitates a composer's music.

Second, EMI analyzes this music using a hierarchical pattern matcher much more elaborate than the one described in Figure 4.13. Motives (or number patterns) are recognized through *size* windowing processes that allow for intervening pitches and other variations, much as those demonstrated in the functions of the previous chapter do. Motives are analyzed in three different ways: pitch alone, rhythm alone, and pitch and rhythm joined. These enable EMI to discover patterns in materials where widely varying pitches or rhythms have been employed for variation. Patterns are weighted by how often they appear, and they are tagged by location. Finally, patterns are recognized within phrases, by phrases, periods, sections, movements, and so forth. Hence, what I call an "image" of a work is formed. An "image" is the result of full-scale pattern recognition in an entire composition.

Third, when two or more images have been completed, EMI superimposes them to reveal two important details. First it discovers which heavily weighted motives are local to a given work (i.e., patterns and variations related only to the thematic peculiarities of one of the stored works) since these will not increase significantly in number during superimposition. Then EMI tags any of the patterns whose number of occurrences has increased significantly in the superimposition. These are then stored in a style dictionary for application during ATN integration. Information about weightings (after the superimposition of the two or more images) and location (i.e., only at cadence, etc.) remains with each pattern or motive.

Next, rules-based composition takes place. This creates styleless music that conforms to traditional melodic, harmonic, and voice-leading rules.

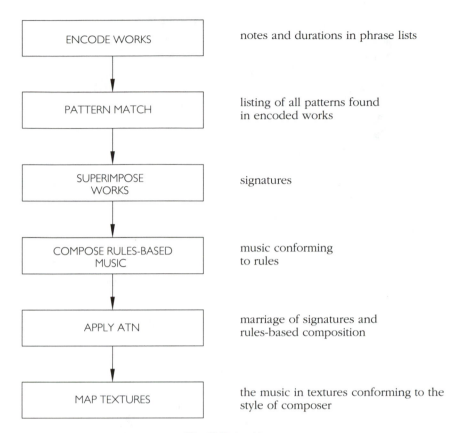

ENCODE WORKS	notes and durations in phrase lists
PATTERN MATCH	listing of all patterns found in encoded works
SUPERIMPOSE WORKS	signatures
COMPOSE RULES-BASED MUSIC	music conforming to rules
APPLY ATN	marriage of signatures and rules-based composition
MAP TEXTURES	the music in textures conforming to the style of composer

FIGURE 5.12   The EMI algorithm.

While not discussed at length here, this process closely parallels traditional part-writing, information about which is already available in music theory textbooks. The program produces context-free phrases in a "Schenker-like" hierarchy (see discussion in Chapter 2). This is accomplished using a top-down composition system. It contributes "correct" tonal music upon which signatures may be inserted similar to countersubjects in `compose-invention` in the last chapter. Most important, it keeps the machine-composed music from becoming intensely saturated with signatures at this stage, which was a problem with the music created by the program of Chapter 4.

The final element, after the translation of notes and durations for performance has taken place, is texture generation. This involves the shaping of the music into one or more voices according to the previously described texture-mapping process. It maps by slimming thick textures or doubling the thin textures provided by the rules-based composition and by allowing signatures that would lose their character if their texture were altered to pass without change.

Figure 5.13 roughly demonstrates this process. In Figure 5.13a and 5.13b, the music is by Mozart. Both 5.13c and 5.13d are EMI-culled motives or pieces of 5.13a and 5.13b respectively. The motives are similar in important ways, though they look different. For example, both melodies land on the beat with the chromatic lower neighboring tone C♯. These then would qualify as signatures in a pattern-matching sequence. In 5.13e a simple tonal melodic line, fairly devoid of style, is shown. This is an example of context-free composition composed by EMI. The theme of 5.13f then shows Mozart's signature grafted melodically into place in the fragment of 5.13e along with an extension. The harmonization in 5.13g was created with a simple implied harmony generator and then in 5.13h paired to fit the normal Mozartean texture. This last example is the main theme of the EMI-composed sonata, third movement, in the style of Mozart (the first movement of which is discussed in the next section).

MOZART SONATA

Completed in the early summer of 1988, the EMI-composed *Sonata* in the style of Mozart follows standard Allegro-Andante-Presto forms. Three Mozart sonatas (K. 283, 309, and 457) were used for signature gathering. These were then applied to machine-composed rules-based composition. Cadences, textures, sequenced gestures, and various ostinati show evidence of derived material, while themes and harmonic progressions demonstrate the influence of specific signatures.

Figure 5.14 shows the entire first movement of the EMI sonata. The overall form is a standard sonata Allegro, with the first theme stated at the outset and the second beginning in bar 22. This second theme is appropriately in the key of the dominant, and it closes the exposition at the traditional repeat sign at the end of measure 35. The development begins in bar 37 with an unusual and abrupt modulation to the parallel minor of the key of the sonata itself. A brief development of the second theme begins in measure 63 in the key of B♭ but is really a sequencing chromatic modulation back to the key of C. The recapitulation begins in measure 72 with the second theme now in the key of C following sonata Allegro traditions. A closing theme begins in measure 107.

I provided the form here by naming upper-level sections. Beyond this the inner structure of cadences and the actual notes were machine-created. The abrupt and unusual modulations obviously demonstrate the

a.

b.

c.

FIGURE 5.13   a) Mozart Sonata No. 1, K. 279,
first movement, mm. 5-8, showing a recurring signature.
b) Mozart Sonata No. 2, K. 280, first movement, mm. 45-46,
also shows a recurring signature.
c) and d) Possible signatures from the previous examples.
e) A new and simple tonal melodic line.
f) The signature grafted melodically into place.
g) Harmony injected through an implied harmony generator.
h) The new music paired to a Mozart-like texture.

d.

e.

f.

g.

FIGURE 5.13   continued.

h.

FIGURE 5.13 continued.

program's weaknesses at the point in time this was composed. The energy of both themes and the vigor of the closing section appear to be strengths.

The character and texture of this movement seem to have been forged out of signatures that "average" those in the available works. As can be seen from Figures 5.15, 5.16, and 5.17, the originals, like the EMI output, all leap around triads (n.b., "tonic" first), often doubled in octaves. The "rocking" quality of the left-hand accompaniment in the computer composition beginning with bar 4 greatly resembles that of Figure 5.16 beginning in its bar 3. The repeated notes of the second bar of EMI's sonata can be found in bars 3–5 of Figure 5.16 and in bars 3 and 4 of Figure 5.17.

Figure 5.18 shows particular cadence types found in Mozart's sonatas. The first nine examples represent six of the many basic cadence types that Mozart uses. Figure 5.18a is a common cadence signature of the period and a particular favorite of Mozart. Here, the leading-tone triad does not resolve when the tonic appears in the bass. The agogic accent, created by the dissonance being four times the duration of the resolution, is a feature quite common in this style. Later variations of this example will show that Mozart rarely varies the dissonance advantage in such relationships. Figure 5.18b shows the standard 4–3 appoggiatura highlighted by grace notes with a trill in the upper voice. Figure 5.18c demonstrates how a 4–3 can be approached by triadic motion in the upper voice and represents a variation of Figure 5.18b. Figure 5.18d shows an ornamentation of the dominant in the upper line before setting up the 4–3 appoggiatura. Figure 5.18e, an elaboration of Figure 5.18a with a quick harmonic rhythm, shows a double

FIGURE 5.14 A machine-composed EMI sonata in the style of Mozart, first movement.

FIGURE 5.14 continued.

FIGURE 5.14   continued.

FIGURE 5.14 continued.

FIGURE 5.14   continued.

FIGURE 5.14 continued.

FIGURE 5.14   continued.

embellishment surrounding the sub-dominant and tonic notes. Figure 5.18f shows a typical two-voice contrary motion with the lower voice moving stepwise and the top leaping triadically.

One important objective of the EMI interface is to observe variants of melodic and harmonic signatures. Figure 5.18g, for example, shows a different voicing for the cadence signature in Figure 5.18a.

The remaining examples show further variants of Figure 5.18a with rhythm and texture the prime areas of deviation. Figure 5.18h shows how voices can converge rather than moving parallel as in the previous example. In Figure 5.18i, the voices move downwards. Figure 5.18j parallels the motion of the Figure 5.18a but with the bass moving first to the dominant and then to the tonic an octave below the initial tonic. In Figure 5.18k,

FIGURE 5.15 From the beginning of Mozart's Sonata No. 5, K. 283.

FIGURE 5.16 The opening measures of Mozart's Sonata No. 7, K. 309.

this same bass lies below a skeletal and less dissonant variation of the signature with only three voices present. Figure 5.18l is more static, and the dominant note is present in the lower staff. In Figure 5.18m, the entire dominant chord appears above the bass note tonic octave. Three other variants are seen in Figures 5.18n–p, with each displaying other changes and combinations typical in Mozart's works. As we have already seen in the

FIGURE 5.17   The beginning of Mozart's Sonata No. 14b, K. 457.

cadences of Figure 2.10e, EMI must be able to recognize such variants and collect them as signatures.

In Figure 5.19 (from Figure 5.14, bars 90–92) one can observe the results of both the generating procedures and the signature interface. Each of the principal elements has some stylistic importance. The signature results from the previously described pattern-matching process. The harmonic, melodic, and rhythmic elements have been derived from rules-based composition. The cadential tonic six-four chord in the second bar is global to tonal music. The right-hand motor pattern is more a Mozartean device, particularly common in two-voice textures. Other composers do not employ it as prevalently as he does. The root position diminished triad in the first bar is more local. Even though it occurs in passing here, it is somewhat more common for Mozart to use this chord in first inversion. The use of melody in the bass voice in octaves occurs in Mozart, though rarely. This is the result of machine composition rather than any style inheritance from the works used for composition. The inversion points out how much Mozart likes to move stepwise in the bass, creating passing inversions and changing states of chords in a slow harmonic rhythm.

It would now be useful to step through the process of creation in order to see the program work in more detail. For this, I will show the evolution of the main theme of the second movement of the same EMI sonata. The theme in Figure 5.20 is a typical example of tonal music of the eighteenth and nineteenth centuries. It was created by EMI without the components for discovering and implanting signatures, developing and implementing texture maps, and other less important controls. The harmonic progression consists of a false start antecedent phrase with a complementary consequent that sequences through a cycle of fifths. The melodic line is imitated in the bass, and the music rhymes with balance at each level. It is not, however, Mozartean.

While musical and at times interesting, the progression is predictable and without focus. After careful reflection, many problems surface. The texture, for example, does not conform to Mozart's lean voicing. There is a decided lack of ornamentation characteristic of Mozart's time. There is an iterative quality to the music. Every level of the sequence is exactly the same, which is very uncharacteristic of the period and the composer. Except for the leading tone in minor, there is a lack of chromatic embellishment common for slow movements in this period. There are no signatures of any kind to help identify this as peculiar to a given composer. Too many notes are repeated, which is very uncharacteristic of Mozart. With the exception of the imitation in the bass voice, one encounters no real feeling of counterpoint so typical in Mozart. There is no (simply stated) "quirkiness" here. Mozart rarely follows the norm. His music is fraught with the unpredictable.

The example in Figure 5.21, while falling somewhat short of full Mozart imitation (slow movements are especially difficult), does show how progress can be made using signatures and ATN. It was created by EMI with all of its components intact. Most of the problems encountered with the previous example have been solved in this opening for the second movement. The results are therefore more consistent with Mozart's style, though not identical. Observe the thin texture, the melodic/harmonic signature at the cadence (here in bar 9; see also Figure 5.18), the heavy imitation, the use of ornaments in the first variation, and so on.

Figure 5.22 shows a few measures from the only 6/8 slow movements in Mozart's piano sonatas and mature concertos. In the first example, the head of the motive is the same as in Figure 5.21, but the leap covers only the interval of a fourth. The second example has a thicker texture and ascends only a third. The last excerpt expands the ascending figure to a sixth (like the EMI composition) but with an interpolated fourth. What is interesting about these examples when compared with the remarkably similar EMI slow movement just presented is that none of them were used at the time of computer composition. Whereas they would make superb examples of successful signature gathering if they had been available at the time of composition, they instead stand as remarkable evidence of computational imitation. The EMI theme was derived from other less obvious Mozart sources through wide-window signature gathering and are a facet of rules-based composition.

FIGURE 5.18   Cadence types found in Mozart's sonatas.
a) Sonata No. 1, K. 279 (1774), second movement, m. 28.
b) Sonata No. 2, K. 280 (1774), first movement, mm. 141-42.
c) Sonata No. 8, K. 311 (1777), second movement, mm. 37-38.
d) Sonata No. 8, K. 311, third movement, m. 165.
e) Sonata No. 18, K. 570 (1789), second movement, m. 4.
f) Sonata No. 1, K. 279 (1774), first movement, mm. 4-5.
g) Sonata No. 2, K. 280 (1774), second movement, mm. 59-60.
h) Sonata No. 3, K. 281 (1774), first movement, m. 40.
i) Sonata No. 5, K. 283 (1774), second movement, m. 39.
j) Sonata No. 5, K. 283, second movement, m. 4.
k) Sonata No. 6, K. 284 (1775), second movement, m. 46.
l) Sonata No. 6, K. 284, third movement, m. 17.
m) Sonata No. 10, K. 330 (1778), first movement, m. 150.
n) Sonata No. 13, K. 333 (1778), first movement, m. 63.
o) Sonata No. 13, K. 333, second movement, last measure.
p) Sonata No. 16, K. 545 (1788), second movement, m. 16.

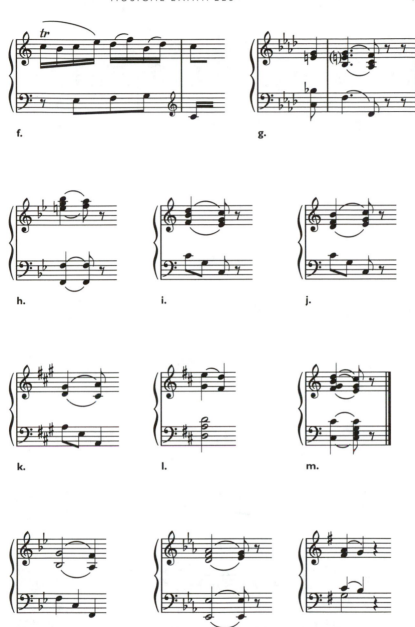

FIGURE 5.18   continued.

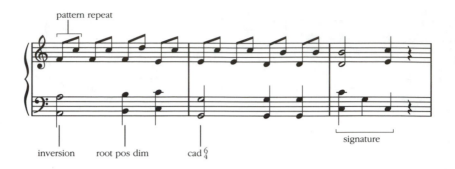

FIGURE 5.19 Bars 90–92 from the EMI sonata in the style of Mozart, first movement, showing derivation.

FIGURE 5.20 Tonal theme without signatures or texture control created by a part of EMI. It represents one possible beginning of a second movement of the sonata shown in Figure 5.14.

FIGURE 5.21 A more likely Mozart imitation using ATN.

JOPLIN RAG

The computer-composed *Rag* (August 1988) in the style of Scott Joplin (Figure 5.25) utilized exactly the same rules-based program as the EMI Bach and Mozart compositions but with a rag form. The special rhythms, harmonic progressions, melodic configurations, and so forth that are reminiscent of Joplin are derived from pattern matching two rags (*Elite Syncopations* and *A Breeze from Alabama*) to extract signatures.

Figures 5.23 and 5.24 show the openings of these works. Each is characterized by an opening in octaves, the syncopation with tied sixteenth notes both across and within beats, and the "um-pah" left-hand figuration

a.   b.

c.

FIGURE 5.22 First measures from Mozart's
a) Sonata No. 2, K. 280 (1774), second movement.
b) Sonata No. 11, K. 331 (1778), second movement.
c) Piano Concerto No. 23, K. 488 (1786), second movement.

in eighth notes. The examples are contrasted in texture and bass line. Each, however, has the indelible mark of Scott Joplin.

EMI took these elements, particularly the ones that occur in both of the Joplin rags, counted them as signatures, and created a new rag. The result, part of which is printed in Figure 5.25, demonstrates the influences of the original works. The opening syncopation of Figure 5.25 (beat 1 of measure 1) seems drawn from the first bar of Figure 5.23 (marked A), a very common Joplin gesture. The second bar of the EMI Joplin example also resembles the rhythm of the first and second bars in Figure 5.23. The pitch pattern of the opening theme of the EMI Joplin appears to be a signature. A detailed comparison of two Joplin excerpts and the EMI opening theme proves quite useful. In order for there to be a signature, matches must exist within the Joplin works themselves. In Figure 5.23, the right hand of bar 1 (notes 3–6, marked A) matches the direction and motion of the right hand of bar 3 of Figure 5.24 (notes 3–6, marked A). Also, the motive that occurs on beat 2 in measure 9 into beat 1 of measure 10 of Figure 5.23 (B) resembles the shape of bar 2 of Figure 5.24 (B), although they have variations past their third notes.

One must realize that with appropriate settings of EMI's pattern-matching parameters, many different forms of the two Joplin motives may

FIGURE 5.23   Opening measures of Scott Joplin's *Elite Syncopations.*

be recognized as matches. These then assure that the result of composition is not simply a pastiche of notes from each piece, but a careful use of the few note groups that stand as signatures. The number of possible variants in a given situation is so high that identifying which groups of notes represent signatures and which represent rules-based composition becomes exhausting and sometimes impossible, even with a listing of signatures for cross-referencing.

PROKOFIEV SONATA

Grappling with quasi-tonal styles demonstrates the effectiveness of the hierarchical approach to machine composition. The harmonic progressions that one finds in the piano music of Sergei Prokofiev might lead one to expect that a fundamental revision of code would be necessary to replicate them. In EMI, however, this is not at all the case. Even though

FIGURE 5.24   Opening measures of Joplin's
A Breeze from Alabama.

this composer's style differs drastically from the music presented so far, only the harmonic ATN part of the program requires alteration. The entire work tree that functions so well for language as well as music stays intact. This substantiates the premise that all music, no matter what the vocabulary, has progressions that are antecedents, consequents, and so forth.

Figure 5.26 shows a typical Prokofiev harmonic progression. To re-create using it, a program would need to have these chords present in the ATN portion of the surface representation. Only data in the chord dictionaries need be changed, not the program itself. Like language, the logical protocol of a syntax can remain intact while different semantic translations change. This is an extremely critical factor in any musical style emulator if it purports to be applicable to different styles including non-tonal ones.

Figure 5.27 presents a computer-generated second movement of a new Prokofiev piano sonata based on the middle movements of his Sonatas No. 3, No. 5, and No. 7. Bars 47–48 of the computer-generated composition

FIGURE 5.25 The beginning section of an EMI Joplin rag.

FIGURE 5.26   A typical Prokofiev harmonic model from his Piano Sonata No. 5, movement 1, bars 177–78.

contain a variant of the progression of Figure 5.26. The beginning of this movement follows closely the triadic accompaniments of both middle movements of Prokofiev's 5th and 7th sonatas. Each has repeating major triads as a backdrop to the main theme. The initial melody resembles that of Peter in Prokofiev's *Peter and the Wolf,* though that was not one of the analyzed works. Like so many similar examples found in the process of automated composition, elements embedded in a composer's style mirror actual works not available to the program during composition.

Figure 5.28 is a notable signature that EMI found during its pattern matching of the above mentioned Prokofiev sonatas. It is found in measures 19–20 of the computer-generated work. The harmonic pattern found in measures 13 (last beat, left hand) and 14 (right hand full measure) of the EMI composition is from measure 112 of movement 1 of Prokofiev's actual Sonata No. 5 (Figure 5.29), with slight variations in octaves (first chord) and voicings. Likewise, measure 113 of Prokofiev's Sonata No. 5, movement 3 (see Figure 5.30), appears in a slightly different guise in its computer-generated counterpart in measure 32 in an inner voice. The accompaniment beginning in measure 38 of the EMI composition appears in Prokofiev's Sonata No. 7 (see Figure 5.31). Each of these signatures required verification from examples in other sonatas much too numerous to describe here.

BALI GAMELAN GONG KEBYAR

Non-Western music offers an extraordinary challenge for analyzing and replicating musical style. A numerical pattern matcher, however, should be able to detect, *without modification*, the same kinds of signatures in non-Western music as it does in the Western European music tradition.

Using the principle that music under study should have a reasonably detectable style (Kessler, Hansen, and Shepard 1984), I chose a musical style from Bali, Indonesia. The word *composer* does not exist in the Balinese language; and, as in many non-Western cultures, works have not been remembered as "by" anyone in particular. Only recently (within the

FIGURE 5.27 A computer-generated second movement of a new Prokofiev piano sonata.

FIGURE 5.27 continued.

FIGURE 5.27   continued.

FIGURE 5.27 continued.

FIGURE 5.27 continued.

FIGURE 5.28 A notable signature from Piano Sonata No. 7, mm. 378–80.

FIGURE 5.29 From measure 112 of movement 1 of Prokofiev's Sonata No. 5.

FIGURE 5.30   Measure 113 of Prokofiev's Sonata No. 5, movement 3, which appears disguised in measure 32 of the EMI composition (Figure 5.27).

FIGURE 5.31   Prokofiev's Sonata No. 7, second movement, m. 38.

last ten years, according to those I have interviewed) have individuals responsible for compositions begun taking credit. Hence, a work from traditional Balinese heritage was chosen rather than a more recent work by a contemporary composer.

I first programmed generic elements of gamelan performance style into the EMI system in lieu of the Western tonal rules-based composition system. Then I visited Bali at length, recording examples of the music and interviewing composers about patterns in their music. Finally, actual examples were encoded for the EMI programs to analyze and imitate. The results were then taped for the reaction of composers in Bali.

Figure 5.32 indicates the high level of pattern repetition that occurs naturally in the traditional Balinese repertoire of gamelan gong kebyar (McPhee 1966). There are many different gamelans (meaning roughly "orchestra") in Bali, of which "gong" is but one. The gamelan of the gong kebyar relies heavily on the use of metallophones (metal xylophones) and the pelog five-note scale and tuning system. The "kebyar" type of composition has been popular in Bali for over fifty years and refers to a dramatic style with sudden changes of dynamics and tempo. Figure 5.33 demonstrates the level of contrast present especially at the outset of gamelan gong kebyar. The bar lines in the figure represent a held silence rather than denoting meter. Hence, the music begins with a giant crash followed by a gaping silence. This is followed by two bursts of rapid-fire homorhythmic gestures separated by silence. This in turn is followed by a highly repetitive section in the top voice (G♯ - A - C♯).

FIGURE 5.32 Patterns in the traditional Balinese repertoire of *gamelan gong kebyar* (after McPhee 1966, p. 345).

FIGURE 5.32 continued

FIGURE 5.32   continued.

FIGURE 5.33   Gamelan gong kebyar showing patterns and their variations.

Both examples demonstrate the five-note scale (roughly C♯ - D - E - G♯ - A), the heavy reliance on patterns and their variations (often three sixteenth notes in a four sixteenth-note per beat metric scheme), as well as the different speeds of the instruments. The patterns (after the lengthy unison introduction), while seemingly repetitive, have subtle variances causing extensive differences in cross-metric accent. Finding any two beats alike in given measures is unlikely. Measures 8 and 9 of Figure 5.32 are the exception to this and provide a brief sense of stability in the otherwise constantly unfolding environment.

FIGURE 5.34   An EMI-composed work based on melodies created by Balinese traditional music.

Figure 5.34 shows an EMI-composed example of music in the style of, if not the *gong kebyar*, at least the gamelan itself. As in the first gamelan example (Figure 5.32), there is no opening chord. Because the work shown in Figure 5.34 is a composite form and a generalization of many, the remainder of the composition is pattern overlay and without pause.

a.   b.   c.

FIGURE 5.35   Signatures from a) Figure 5.32. b) Figure 5.33.
c) Figure 5.34.

Elements of style are found in the intricate sixteenth pattern of voice two, the interlocking patterns of voice two and voice one, and the eight-beat gong cycle (seven beats of rest and one beat of struck low gong). Signatures abound in the EMI example. Most noteworthy of these is the half-step, whole-step motion upwards. This is shown in Figure 5.35. The pattern in Figure 5.35a occurs many times in Figure 5.32 (middle line), shifting its relation to the beat. The pattern in Figure 5.35b occurs in the upper voice of Figure 5.33, from the middle of the work on. It begins on many different parts of the beat, as does the pattern (shown in Figure 5.35c) in the middle voice of the EMI-composed work (Figure 5.34). The difference in pitch content between the latter example and the first two is related to machine performance, not to anything substantive.

Aside from the facts that a notation barrier must be crossed before encoding can begin and that tremendous cultural characteristics are missing by default, machine composing non-Western music (at least that of Bali) seems, on the surface, almost as successful as creation of Western traditional music. No major changes in code are required to have the machine compose in a style similar to Mozart's or in one similar to that of Bali. Signatures surface immediately in both.

Responses from composers that I interviewed in Bali confirm that machine-composed Balinese gamelan music falls tolerably and sometimes quite acceptably within their definitions of the gamelan genre. As with their Western counterparts, Balinese listeners differ in whether machine-composed gamelan music imitates the genre successfully. So much depends on the performers' style of improvisation, which will vary from performance to performance.

What is noteworthy here is that when instrumentation, tuning, and scale types are stripped away from both Western and Balinese music, they resemble each other to a surprising degree. Patterns are evident everywhere and at various levels of composition. Signatures abound in both types of music and in the machine-composed examples. Of course, the study of just one type of music could not be considered an adequate sampling of the wide diversity of music throughout the world. It may be that my own disposition toward certain Western and non-Western musics has deeply biased the entire comparison. Only time and further research can tell us.

COUNTERPOINT

Contrapuntal music poses serious problems to machine composition. It would seem that rule-ridden structures such as canons and fugues would be quite suited to digital replication. However, these forms require tremendous amounts of skill to avoid continually backtracking and restarting compositions led astray by a series of correct contrapuntal answers leading to situations in which there are no right possibilities. As well, many contrapuntal forms have varied amounts of freedom depending on the section of the composition. The exposition of a fugue, for example, is highly structured. Fugue developments on the other hand are often quite free.

The first major problem facing a program attempting to create new works in a particular style in a rigorous contrapuntal form is the selection of an appropriate theme or subject. Whereas in non-contrapuntal composition a good theme is a good theme, in strict counterpoint, some good themes work much better than others. It could even be said that many bad themes work better than many good themes. Subjects that stick to stepping or leaping are likely to hold their identity better in the deeper textures of the middle of a work than those that are a mixture of the two. Likewise, subjects that have regular and predictable harmonic rhythms, especially those that flip-flop back and forth between tonic and dominant, work better than those that don't. Then there is the intuitive factor that comes only with the advent of great skill that a lifetime of writing in such a form provides. Many of these elements can be programmed. Others, especially the last, cannot.

The first example of machine composition of a contrapuntal form is shown in Figure 5.36. This work was modeled after parts of a single work by Palestrina, the beginning of which is shown in Figure 5.37. Note the similar delayed entrances and the manner of imitation at various octaves and fifths. Most of this is rules-driven—the approach was not inherited from the model but written in the form of instructions to the program, which are similar to (but more complex than) the code described in the section on add-second-voice in Chapter 4. Since the individual lines are treated both as repeated melodic voices *and* as members of constituent harmonies, the number of rules is approximately twice the number required for composition in which harmony and melody are separate elements.

FIGURE 5.36 The beginning of an EMI Kyrie in the style of Palestrina.

FIGURE 5.37 From Palestrina's Agnus Dei I from the *Pope Marcellus Mass.*

The beginning of such compositions represents the most difficult hurdle since the formalism of staggered entrances and the choice of octave in which a voice begins are critical to the success of the composition. Once begun, however, the music becomes less restricted, with exact imitations spliced in with freer composition. Obviously, the form is more exact than described here. Nonetheless, the appearance of the style of Palestrina is present in the computer-composed musical example.

The composition of a fugue in the style of Bach is quite a different matter indeed. The fugue exposition is particularly difficult for even the best of composers. Computer programs, however, can work effectively, albeit slowly, in this type of constraint-based environment.

The opening of an EMI-composed fugue is shown in Figure 5.38. The theme is diatonic and once begun is driven principally by sixteenth notes. The second entry in the alto voice is a fifth up from the original (a requirement of the form) and is "tonal." This means that instead of leaping a fifth as the original does, it leaps back to the tonic note of the key. This is also a requirement of the form. The third entrance occurs in the soprano voice. It returns to the original fifth but transposed an octave upwards. The final entrance returns to the tonal schema of a fourth and leads to the end of the fugal exposition.

All of this strict imitation must also fit the harmonic functions. In bar 4, it becomes clear that the harmonic rhythm for this theme moves typically at a rate of one chord per beat. Most of the chords here are tonic, dominant, and sub-dominant and as such follow tonal harmonic protocols that allow for standard voice leading. Again, this is rules-based as it was in the

FIGURE 5.38 The opening of an EMI fugue in the style of Bach.

FIGURE 5.39   The beginnings of Bach's Fugue a) No. 8 and b) No. 9 from *Das Wohltemperierte Klavier.*

`compose-invention` program described in the previous chapter. The computer did not inherit any of this from the models on which it is based—that would be an extraordinary feat that EMI is most certainly not capable of in its current incarnation. Fugue "rules" were programmed and then signatures and context-free composition caused to fit into those rules.

The brief movement to the key of G major in bar 5 is part of the structure provided in the rules. Most Bach fugues have chromaticism, modulation, or both before this point. However, it was deemed difficult enough to work with the constraint set for fugue writing without extending the algorithm to include such interesting but complicating features. The machine was also instructed to create a constantly driving sixteenth-note composite rhythm to help evoke the Baroque "motor" rhythm. The first quasi-fugue to emerge from EMI did not have such a rule and sounded very much out of style.

Figure 5.39 shows the beginning of two of the Bach fugues on which the composition of the previous figure was based. The first, Figure 5.39a, shows a good example of a "tonal" second entry. The second example, Figure 5.39b, shows both the more typical real answer chromaticism as well as the sixteenth-note motor rhythm given in the EMI fugue. All of the fugue models were taken from *Das Wohltemperierte Klavier.* Examples of three- and four-voice fugues were included for signature gathering. The number of voices in the EMI composition was dictated by the rules given in the program and were not a part of any inheritance taking place.

In EMI, at least, counterpoint is a special case. The program simply cannot adapt to the new environment without some serious new code. Composing in Renaissance counterpoint (as with the Palestrina example) or more rigid fugal forms requires programs, similar to that explained in Chapter 4 for invention-like counterpoint, that enable signatures and context-free composition to be layered into the constraint structure.

FURTHER EXAMPLES

Performance aspects in the field of computer music as a whole never seem more critical than when dealing with automated and computer-assisted composition, where one is usually working with synthetic or sampled sounds simultaneously with a composition using those sounds. Such is the case with Figure 5.40, a machine-composed chorale in the style of J. S. Bach. The "sampled" vocal sounds with which this music was first played were so without life and substance that it was almost thrown away. Subsequent live performance proved it to be a highly effective replication in the style of Bach.

This chorale is particularly noteworthy in that the incipient melodic line begins in much the same way as Bach's "Christ lag in Todesbanden" (Cantata No. 4, Figure 5.41a) which was not one of the chorales available to the program at the time of composition. However, the chorales shown in Figure 5.41b–d, which have similar openings, were analyzed. The part writing in the EMI composition follows the rules of the common practice period since most of the actual composition is the direct result of context-free rules-based composition (i.e., few, if any, signatures). Bach's chorale style represents the foundation for much of the voice-leading rules of the common practice period. Hence few pattern-matching impregnations need to be made in order to make the music sound in the style of the composer.

Pattern matching seems to work well when dealing with composers with a definable style consisting of motives repeated from work to work. It obviously becomes less and less successful the more adventuresome and quirky the style. Such is the case with Carl Philipp Emanuel Bach's sonatas for flute and continuo. The small signature dictionary created from freely matching these works had to be plumbed to the fullest in order for composition to take place at all. The music starts and stops irregularly, is sometimes very chromatic and other times diatonic, and, more important, seems to lack commonality between compositions except for this tendency for sudden change.

Figure 5.42 gives some indication of this. The flute line is rhythmically quite diverse (thirty-second to quarter notes). The continuo part is less

FIGURE 5.40 An EMI-composed chorale in the style of J.S. Bach.

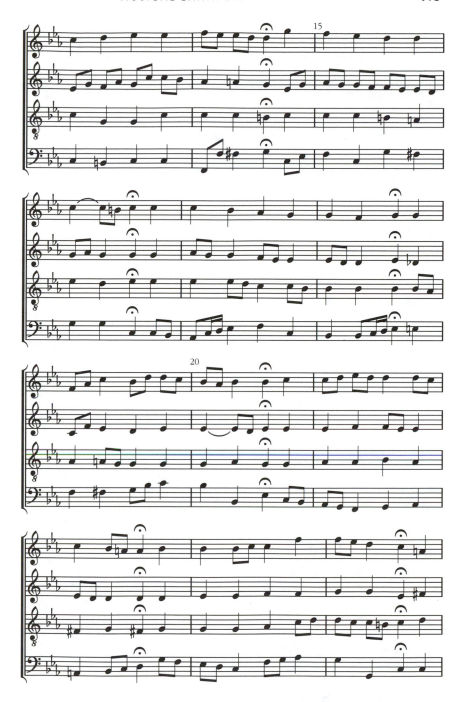

FIGURE 5.40 continued.

FIGURE 5.40   continued.

relevant since it was created from chord symbols by an editor. The piece moves from the tonic G to the dominant within two and one-half measures. The harmonic rhythm changes from eighth-note motion to quarter-note motion almost randomly (certainly not a characteristic this composer would have in common with his father, J. S. Bach).

EMI found few signatures from matching this work with the others in the series (four in all were used). As can be seen from the replicant of Figure 5.43, the major effect of the matching was less in the way of signatures and more in the way of generalized gestures. For example, the opening rhythm and repeated notes are something one finds in every composer's music. In Figure 5.43, however, it seems to have been almost copied from the original. Note the early modulation in the computer attempt as well as the wide leaps (a characteristic of C. P. E. Bach's style, though not shown in Figure 5.42).

Linda Burman-Hall and Leta Miller, who commissioned this particular work for a Baroque music concert, declared after the first rehearsal that

FIGURE 5.41 The beginnings of Bach chorales
a) No. 184, "Christ lag in Todesbanden."
b) No. 294, "Herr Jesu Christ, du höchstes Gut."
c) No. 218, "Laß, o Herr, dein Ohr sich neigen."
d) No. 215, "Verleih' uns Frieden gnädiglich."

FIGURE 5.42   From C. P. E. Bach's Sonate G-dur (1739).

this music "was more like P. D. Q. Bach than C. P. E." This is no doubt due to the lack of available signatures, the above-mentioned diversity of the music, and the banal attempts by the computer to match larger structural issues such as abrupt modulations and inconsistent rhythmic and harmonic motions. EMI returns as much style as it finds and in this case found little of consequence.

A final issue regards performance practice itself. So much of the style here is found in the performance realm. Based on traditions of the period, performers vary the ornamentation, accompaniment, and phrasing in certain distinct manners and instill rubato according to practices of the time. Thus, in final performance the work was not an embarrassment and, while not as convincing as other works produced by the EMI program, seemed musically interesting.

Performance practice also plays a significant role in the next work to be discussed: an EMI-composed mazurka in the style of Frederic Chopin. Mazurkas pose a significant challenge to computer composition since so much of the actual style is imparted through their interpretation. An

FIGURE 5.43 The beginning of a sonata for flute and continuo in the style of C. P. E. Bach.

FIGURE 5.43 continued.

example of this occurs when the metric accent is shifted from the first beat to the second and (less often) the third beat. Chopin does not often indicate this explicitly, except for occasional missing down beats or ornamentation on beats other than the first. This discriminates mazurkas from waltzes, for example, which have strong down beats. As well, the rhythm is more flexible in performance since a piano mazurka is not performed as a dance. These elements are not found explicitly notated in the original Chopin works and hence are not available for style replication.

Four of the fifty-one Chopin mazurkas (Op. 17, No. 1; Op. 33, No. 2; Op. 67, No. 3; Op. 68, No. 3) were used for the EMI composition shown in Figure 5.44. It has a three-part form, with the middle section (bar 24) significantly contrasting with the first, as is generally the case with such works. Note the resemblance of the beginning theme to Chopin's own in Figure 5.45a, and compare the middle section theme with Figure 5.45b. Pattern matching, as with the C. P. E. Bach, was liberal rather than exact.

The triplets in this example were derived solely from the Mazurka Op. 33, No. 2 by Chopin in combination with context-free composition. Triplets are not prevalent in Chopin's mazurkas. It seems this compositional anomaly is almost a machine invention rather than a derivative. Such

FIGURE 5.44   An EMI mazurka in the style of Frederic Chopin.

FIGURE 5.44   continued.

FIGURE 5.44 continued.

a.

b.

FIGURE 5.45 From Chopin's a) Mazurka Op. 67, No. 3, and
b) Mazurka Op. 68, No. 3.

accidents often serve to enhance rather than detract from the novelty of machine composition as they provide surprises in an otherwise somewhat predictable environment of signatures, especially if the latter are overused.

Even though an excellent piano sample was used in the original performance of Figure 5.44, it did not help the metric rigidity of machine performance, which is sterile and cannot be relied on for evaluating the quality of machine composition. Live performance, however, proved this to be a highly effective re-creation of Chopin's mazurka style. This included all of the aforementioned performance practice mazurka indicators as well as dynamic nuances and pedaling.

The next example, an EMI intermezzo in the style of Brahms (see Figure 5.46), is the result of pattern matching an amalgam of different piano works of Brahms. Thus the resultant form (not shown in its entirety here) is an average of those presented in Brahms's intermezzi, waltzes, ballades, and rhapsodies. As well, many of those chosen (see particularly his Ballade in B major, Op. 10, No. 4, Waltz Op. 39, No. 9, and Rhapsody in G minor, Op. 79, No. 2) have uncharacteristically thin textures compared to his more usual rich and fecund accompaniments. Hence, the resultant machine composition's texture is relatively barren compared to what one might think a work by Brahms might look like. Hearing it, however, gives a much different impression as the steady driving rhythm and set accompaniment give immediate rise to the impression of Brahms's style. The main theme seems to interlock the theme of Figure 5.47a and the accompaniment of Figure 5.47b. This points out the fact that a musical ATN allows for accompaniments to be separated from melodies and then attached to other melodies provided appropriate harmonic changes occur. One line is influenced by a similar line in Brahms, while its accompaniment is generated from an accompaniment found in an entirely different work.

The next example, like the Palestrina of Figure 5.37, requires special attention to work size. George Gershwin composed only three preludes (published in 1927) of which only one is slow in tempo (No. 2). Since a slow prelude was desired, this made matters even more difficult. The solution was found in splitting up the work and pretending that each part was an original complete work by Gershwin. What is gained in doing this is that the resultant pattern match is rich in local signatures. What is lost is that these signatures may be so local as to be identifiable exclusively with this one prelude (that is, we get only a slight variation of the original). Recognition of form is lost as well.

Figure 5.48 is EMI's second attempt at creating a new prelude in the style of Gershwin. The first was an example of the slight variation mentioned above and hence not a version I would be proud to print. This second attempt shows the second problem mentioned above, however:

FIGURE 5.46 The opening of an EMI-composed intermezzo in the style of Johannes Brahms.

FIGURE 5.46 continued.

FIGURE 5.47 From a) Waltz Op. 39, No. 9.
b) Capriccio in B minor Op. 76, No. 2, by Johannes Brahms.

the form is a mutilation of that which we know today to be "blues," something very much retained by Gershwin but lost here because of the fracturing of one work into many. This is seen in the seventeen-bar length of the main theme of Figure 5.48. Since "blues" have generally twelve-bar main themes (a sixteen-bar theme is also possible), the theme in Figure 5.48 is immediately recognized for its non-blues length and pattern by those who know the style.

A portion of the original Gershwin model is shown in Figure 5.49. The main theme is twelve bars (the introduction has been left out). Bars 5–12 and bars 8–16 are treated as separate small works. This method of chunking the work into small pieces allows for style recognition at one level (signature) and not at another (form). Interestingly, the idea of beefing

FIGURE 5.48   The beginning of an EMI-composed prelude in the style of George Gershwin.

FIGURE 5.48 continued.

up the theme the second time it is played (see Figure 5.48) does appear as a formal idiom in the Gershwin. But this occurs in the new work no doubt due more to built-in rules about form in general than any inheritance from the available work.

Using examples from Béla Bartók's *Mikrokosmos* posed particular problems for the EMI program, as did the Stravinsky in the next chapter. Not only is Bartók's style quasi-tonal, and thus more difficult for creating rules-based composition in which to implant signatures, but it uses unusual (for classical traditions) meters and accent arrangements within those meters. The solution for both of these problems was to choose like-metered and like-sounding examples to analyze in order to use more signatures in composition. As well, the pattern matcher itself was given instructions to match more freely. While not a good idea in tonal music (since doing so produces many non-signatures), this idea seems to have worked well in this instance.

Figure 5.50 shows the beginning of the results of an EMI attempt to compose in Bartók's piano style. While not eminently successful, the

FIGURE 5.49   From the second of George Gershwin's three preludes.

music does show a number of stylistic characteristics of works in the *Mikrokosmos*. The 7/8 meter, for example, is resident in both portions of the works shown in Figure 5.51. As well, the texture of Figure 5.51b shows up substantially in the EMI-composed music. Finally, the switching of textures between hands seems to come as an overshadowing of the two examples of Bartók, with the first providing the idea of interplay and the second the idea of melody on top.

Elements of style that did not surface in the machine replication are chromaticism (of which both of the Bartók works have an abundance) and

FIGURE 5.50   From an EMI-composed *Kosmos* in the style of Béla Bartók.

a real sense of direction. While this latter commodity is somewhat personal, it is clear that the machine work is simply stagnant, while the real Bartók is vibrant with direction. Obviously it is possible to expect too much from a machine, especially when one of the main components, context-free composition, is no longer allowed to operate effectively during the compositional process.

FIGURE 5.51   From Béla Bartók's *Mikrokosmos:*
a) "Scherzo" (Book 3, No. 82).
b) "Six Dances in Bulgarian Rhythm" (Book 6, No. 149, mm. 50–53).

BIBLIOGRAPHY

Cope, David. "A Computer Model of Music Composition." In *Machine Models of Music*, Stephan Schwanauer and David Levitt, eds. Cambridge, Mass.: MIT Press, 1991.

Kessler, Edward, Christa Hansen, and Roger Shepard. "Tonal Schemata in the Perception of Music in Bali and in the West." *Music Perception* 2,2 (Winter 1984): 131–165.

McPhee, Colin. *Music in Bali*. New Haven: Yale University Press, 1966.

COMPUTER-ASSISTED COMPOSITION

. . . .

INTRODUCTION

To this point, the text has focused on machine composition. While this requires users to build databases, no integral interaction between the program and user takes place. In many instances, such interaction would be advantageous. Interfaces wherein users can be assisted by the machine without it creating entire works are therefore helpful. This is most important when working with complicated non-tonal styles of the twentieth century as well as when creating new works in the user's style.

This chapter will focus on a number of ways to accomplish these goals. The first to be discussed is the possibility of accessing what the SPEAC system considers viable musical representations. Then the chapter describes a series of methods that mix, circumvent, or alter databases before composition takes place. Lastly, original composition is discussed as it relates to me as a composer.

NON-TONAL EQUIVALENTS TO FUNCTION

Any replicative system that is able to generate new context-sensitive works from a context-free environment has advantages. Most

FIGURE 6.1   Examples of functions of tonic–dominant–tonic with very different surface qualities.

important of these is the ability to exchange surface data so that composing functions can remain intact, even when one is composing music in non-tonal styles (Fry 1984). Conceptually, this has significant ramifications. Musical "dominants" can remain as tied to "tonics" as they do in all tonal music.

In fact the entire SPEAC system (discussed in Chapter 2) may operate without alteration. What the identifiers *mean*, however, changes. For example, the familiar C – E – G of the C-major tonic chord could be changed to C – C♯ – D. This implies more than just simple substitution. Harmonic styles could become extremely dissonant. The logic of the system would remain intact, however, and chord functions would be audible even though the surface qualities of the music were very different. Dominant chords, represented as any conglomerate of pitches, would be as recognizable as in tonal music if such recognition were the result of contextual repetition and location in time.

Figure 6.1 shows three different forms of the progression tonic–dominant–tonic, each one having very different surface qualities. The SPEAC system, however, suggests that these examples are equivalent in functional interpretation, not contrasting. While each of the examples varies significantly from the others, the consistency of technique of use, cadential placement, and repetition would allow each to have the fullest meaning of tonic–dominant–tonic in a tonal sense. Conversely, lack of repetition or location sensitivity results in each becoming functionless. Even the neighboring motion in the first, the most common form of tonal motion, can be forced into situations in which function has little relevance (i.e., the minimalists' use of repetition without tonal focus). Much of the perception of "tonalness," of course, is in the ear of the beholder. If one is unprepared to accept non-triadic function in music, one will not hear non-triadic function in music, even if it is there.

Other tonal-based systems have proven to be useful in working with non-tonal or quasi-non-tonal musics (Narmour 1977). The Schenkerian approach, thought by many to be a strictly tonal concept, can be applied to

FIGURE 6.2 A Schenkerian analysis of the opening measures of Igor Stravinsky's *Symphony in Three Movements.* This reduction is based on one done by Felix Salzer (1962).

non-tonal or quasi-tonal musics with fruitful results. In the work by Stravinsky, analyzed in Figure 6.2, functions are shown to exist even in non-triadic vertical sonorities. The same reductive, layer-by-layer analysis proves equally useful in Stravinsky's music as it does in the Schenkerian analysis of a Bach chorale (Figure 2.6).

Prolongation, in the form of repeated motives centering on certain pitch conglomerates, can be seen (and heard) as a factor of foreground incidence and not background meaning. In the music of composers as distinct as Bach and Stravinsky, with Stravinsky at the limits of tonality, chord *grammar* and chord *significance* have distinctively separate meanings. The latter relies on *function*, while the former dictates the succession rules in current use.

Using these principles, I substituted chord dictionaries while maintaining the same tonal grammar discussed in Chapter 2 in the creation of a small quartet in the style of Igor Stravinsky. The results (shown in Figure

6.3) demonstrate the potential of a system with the rules separated from data. Note how the succession protocol has little reference to tonal vocabularies. Rather, it depends on a kind of inherent rhetoric that seems applicable to the style of Stravinsky. Dissonances abound, but from the perspective of hierarchical functional analysis, these chords simply substitute as equivalents for triads. The fragmentary and heavily motivic middle portion of this replication exemplifies the notion of signature development.

The replication of complex twentieth-century music is made possible by understanding the relevance of interpolated surface structures in nested hierarchical prolongations. To rewrite programs in order to accommodate music that, however different it may sound, is fundamentally related to Western tradition would be contrary to logic. Exchanging databases and utilizing the same rules base is the more attractive and illuminating approach.

VARYING THE INTERPRETER PROTOCOLS

In EMI, one may vary the interpreter protocols. This is accomplished by changing the orderings shown in Chapter 2. This has the effect in tonal music of establishing new arrangements of chords so that tonic need not follow dominant. It can force new logic into non-tonal musics.

The work in Figure 6.4, *For Keith*, represents computer-assisted composition on a facetious but effective level. For this composition, various computer compositions have been overlaid in the fashion of Ives to create a mosaic of musical styles made all the more interesting the more familiar the listener is with the quoted works. The right hand of bars 1–5, for example, are the opening five bars of the EMI Mozart sonata found in Chapter 5, while the left hand plays portions of the EMI Bach invention found elsewhere in that same chapter (transposed in *For Keith* to C major). The right hand of bars 6–8, on the other hand, are from the EMI Joplin rag (see bars 5–10 of that work in Chapter 5) juxtaposed with the left-hand of bars 3–5 of voice three of the EMI Bach fugue. The work continues in like manner, producing an economic one minute's worth of computer-composed music.

Another form of computer-assisted composition is found in the work *Mozart in Bali*, shown in Figure 6.5. This work is entirely machine-composed, but the database has been changed during composition. Hence, what begins in a fairly recognizable Mozartean, or at least classical, style, ends in a fairly recognizable Balinese gamelan style. Between these two

FIGURE 6.3 An EMI-composed *Quartet* for woodwind instruments in the style of Stravinsky.

FIGURE 6.3   continued.

FIGURE 6.4 *For Keith,* based on computer-composed compositions overlaid in the fashion of Ives.

FIGURE 6.4   continued.

extremes is a slow transition in which the Alberti bass repeated pattern converts to a more Balinese-like interlocking motive. The recognition process can be assisted by an equally interesting gradual change of timbres from piano at the beginning to sounds very much like gamelan metallophones at the end. Like the change in pitch content, this would happen through a slow transition that would follow the slow change of range. In performance, I used a sampler with gamelan bells set to pelog tuning (one of the scales of Indonesian music).

A third type of computer-assisted composition involves the use of music from two or more composers placed in a single database. One resultant composition, while entirely machine-composed, is an amalgam of signatures that two composers have in common. The *Freeman Quartet* is dedicated to Betty Freeman, whose invitation for an EMI concert at her house first provoked the question of style combinations. In Figure 6.6, works by J. S. Bach (several chorales and inventions) and Samuel Barber (the *Adagio for Strings*—from which the form, as well as stylistic elements, were derived) were combined to form a single database.

The principal melodic line in the first violin provides an obvious example of the result of the mixture of styles. Here, the first six intervals are a third or less in size (five are major or minor seconds), following the melodic conservatism of Bach. In contrast, two of the next three intervals are a sixth or larger. Harmonically, the first three beats of the first measure shown here are the same G-minor triad, while the last beat extends this to a more Barber-like minor-minor seventh chord.

VACUUM GENESIS AND THE MORNING OF THE WORLD

The EMI system is designed for computer-assisted as well as automatic composition. The system is halted at the end of various levels

FIGURE 6.5   *Mozart in Bali,* an entirely machine-composed
example with the database switched during composition.

FIGURE 6.5 continued.

FIGURE 6.6 From the *Freeman Quartet.*

FIGURE 6.6   continued.

of the compositional process and not continued until desired. In the meantime, users have access to all of the data thus far composed and may alter them in any manner.

Figure 6.7 is the opening of the first movement of *Vacuum Genesis*. This composition is based on sections like Figure 6.8 from my *Concert for Piano and Orchestra* (1979; see bibliography). The inheritance of repeated notes along with scattered attacks can be seen. The wide leaps of the *Concert*, however, were apparently not observed as a signature, and hence the computer output is more restrained and stays within a tritone in Figure 6.7.

Figure 6.9 is page 7 of the published score of the fourth movement of *Vacuum Genesis*. Working with EMI is entirely "top down." This means that the program stops at various levels, allowing the user access to the data. The top level of the composing process appears first as a set of sections with contrasting music in each. The delay is indefinite, so that users can spend days in testing, listening to, and revising the material.

Second, material is inherited as the process proceeds so that changes made in the single section at a high level will be found again in repeating sections as phrases are born. Changes can then be made to the repeating sections to make them yet further variations of original themes.

Third, and possibly most important, the ATN factor may alter the user's changes. In effect, competing forces will be at work, constantly mapping and overriding data in the work being composed. While simpler programs could avoid these seeming contradictions, the competing forces often produce some of the finer surprises of the computer-assisted composition thus far produced. A human change of computer-composed music at one level may be altered by the ATN at another level, producing interesting

FIGURE 6.7   From the first movement of *Vacuum Genesis*, a machine-composed work in the style of the author.

side effects that can be shaped more elegantly by further human alter-ations, which can then be partially or totally altered by the computer at yet another level. Luckily, the program remembers *all* of the material com-posed at each level, meaning that whenever ATN obliterates some or all of the music at one level, the preceding material can be retrieved and re-implanted at the next level.

Fourth, users may change part or all of the current database at any time during the process of computer-assisted composition. Depending on the amount of change and the nature of the changes themselves, this can dramatically affect the flow and ideas of a work in progress. The system was designed to include contrast in the compositional process, but con-trast that is relevant and subtle. Switching databases with wildly different

FIGURE 6.8   A section from the author's *Concert for Piano and Orchestra*, upon which *Vacuum Genesis* was based.

materials, even styles, can create dynamic contrasts like switching timbres from piano to sitar.

Finally, the user has access not only to the music at a given level but also to all the other elements. Hence, identifiers can be changed, even functions can be replaced with other functions, causing tremendous changes in the production of music at the next level. Logically, the more one knows about how the system operates, the more effectively these changes can be made. Certainly, the more changes made, the more dynamic the compositional process becomes, and the more defined the computer–human relationship becomes. The computer processes immense amounts of data

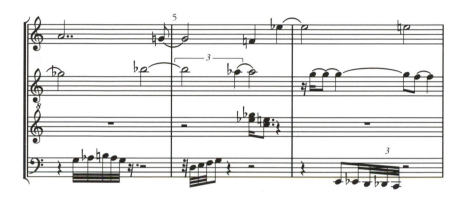

FIGURE 6.9 From the published score of the fourth movement of *Vacuum Genesis.*

quickly and accurately, while the human partner uses instinct, intuition, and personal aesthetics to judge and revise the results.

This is evident in the computer-assisted creation of a string trio (violin, viola, violoncello) in my style: *The Morning of the World.* The title is the phrase that India's Prime Minister Nehru was supposed to have used in describing Bali when he first arrived there in the 1950s. The form and choice of exact database were created while I was in Bali. The database used for this work was based on long passages found in four-line reductions of my *Concert for Piano and Orchestra.* These reductions were treated as if they were complete works in themselves. The passages chosen were based on similarities found between them. The desired result was a consistently chromatic yet quasi-tonal vocabulary with Cope signatures abounding.

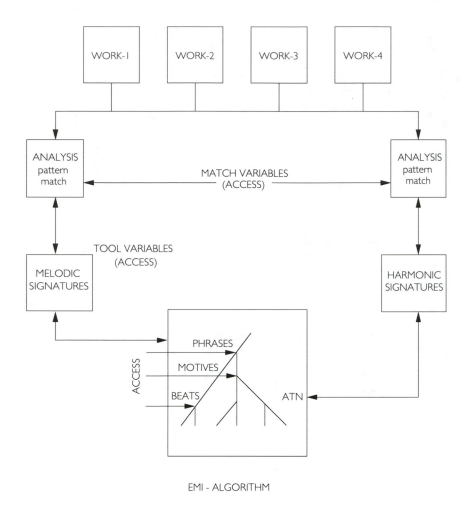

EMI - ALGORITHM

FIGURE 6.10 EMI set for computer-assisted composition.

The computer-assisted process in EMI is variable by depth; that is, one may wish to step through the process at progressively smaller levels. Hence, variables were devised to give users the opportunity to have access to the composing process at each level. One variable, for example, accesses the principal composing function itself so that one can view and change the first two phrases of the work before the next two are born.

Figure 6.10 shows a layout of the entire EMI system when set for computer-assisted use. The higher-level functions run with default arguments (i.e., have no user-called arguments), while lower sets of functions provide more opportunity for inputting compositional variables. This is typical of EMI's programs. The more knowledge you have of the programs and the programming language, the more accessible the arguments become for variations.

To give the reader some indication what an EMI database looks like musically requires a sampling of the music from the *Concert for Piano and Orchestra* (see Figure 6.11). Observe the dependence on counterpoint in this example. My music relies on a consistent interplay of voices rather than on more typical melodic-harmonic models. Melody is often the result of a combination of voices rather than the pronounced independence of a single line with others subservient to a harmonic role. Cadences, climaxes, and incipient gestures are derived rhythmically as much as harmonically. As well, the style constantly hints at tonality without being explicitly tonal. Dissonance resolves even as it produces subsequent dissonances.

As previously mentioned, as a consequence of a desire for increased continuity and consistency, I fooled EMI's programs by breaking the passage even further (it is already a section of a larger piece) into four sub-sections, each with its own integrity. Also, since the desired output required a trio rather than a quartet, the actual data was reduced to three voices. Little of the music was lost, however, since, with the exception of a few places, voices do not move together, and rests often create a three-voice texture in the original.

The next stage of the compositional process requires the setting of variables to what I believe to be reasonable amounts. Depending on one's experience both with the system and with the musical style under study, this can take varying amounts of time. At its briefest, one can simply rely on the default settings that the variables have when EMI is initialized. In the extreme (i.e., fine tuning), one would take care to arrest the composing process at a very fine level to observe parts of phrases and then retune them based on listening. At this point, one simply corrects the material created and resets one of the variables depending on the circumstance or, if the sample is too out of style, rejects it and begins again at the previous level.

The Morning of the World was composed during a controlled computer-assisted composing session. The results are shown in Figure 6.12. Observe the signature of one eighth plus two sixteenth notes in the viola and cello lines (beat 4 of bar 1) that occurs four times during this example. The small and consistent database allows for extreme focus on such gestures, which is not possible with the inclusion of more diverse works, where likely signatures would not so easily appear in the pattern-matching process.

FIGURE 6.11   Several measures from the *Concert for Piano and Orchestra* by the author.

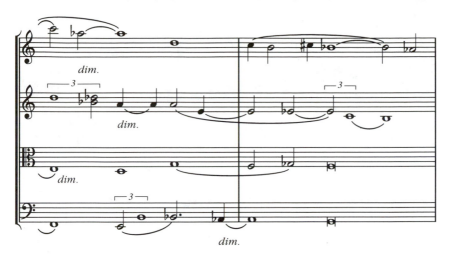

FIGURE 6.11   continued.

After several performances both by machine and by hand at various keyboards, I noted several points that did not fulfill my aesthetic preferences (circled in the figure). These unfulfilling areas centered on material too consonant for my taste and music far too dissonant for the context. Hence, I simply "fixed" the notation in order for the music to translate into Figure 6.13.

After several further performances to ensure my tastes had been met, I then re-entered the compositional sequence with the previous composed material and started up the composing sequence again. In EMI this is accomplished by removing the first identifier in the default sequence of arguments (meaning that there is one less phrase to be composed) and attaching the file of already composed music to the removed identifier's property list.

The results of the second composition run are shown in Figure 6.14. Note the now out-of-octave signature present in the first period as well as the use of scales provided by the contrast-generating aspect of the program. The circled locations for change indicate my displeasure with problems of (1) range, (2) diatonic scaling, and (3) simplicity of chord structure. As well, certain functional repeats (evidenced in bar 7) offer a lack of purposeful variety. The changes shown in Figure 6.15 make this passage a successful (in my mind) variation of the machine-composed version of a second theme.

Space does not permit a full-scale rendition of the final results of the computer-assisted composition of the string trio. However, it should be

FIGURE 6.12   A section of *The Morning of the World* with problems circled.

evident from the examples presented that the compositional process is dynamic and constantly productive. The machine-composed music is often interesting, filled with problems, provocative, and rarely discarded.

Ultimately, potential users of systems like EMI will prefer linear programs and more interactive environments. One can imagine a system wherein users simply perform naturally on their instruments with the computer program keeping track of both the current state of the work being improvised and the broader sweep of style of the composer. Anytime computer-composed music is desired, it can be called and performed immediately. Such requests could be due to composer's block or just for

FIGURE 6.13 "Fixed" music from Figure 6.12.

curiosity. It could be in any amount, from a single pitch to the rest of the work at hand. The music could then be manipulated directly from the instrument.

Such imaginings are not far from reality. As programming environments become more user friendly they will also become more attuned to interfaces that connect with their owner's expertise. With the control of nuance and other matters, such programs would become the perfect composing partner, working hand-in-hand with composers to achieve the best and most musical results.

Finally, one can imagine systems such as EMI with reflexive variables that evaluate their failures and retune or even revise code. Such programs

FIGURE 6.14   A second run of *The Morning of the World*
with problems circled.

would truly emulate musical *intelligence* (Winston 1984). For now, we will
have to be content with successes in computer analysis and replication of
musical style.

THE FUTURE

Style replication, whether it be for computer-assisted extensions of personal composition or for creating new works in the styles

FIGURE 6.15   A final version of a second theme for *The Morning of the World.*

of composers long since dead, is still very much in its infancy. Whatever the success of EMI, works still suffer from problems of continuity, stylistic anomalies, and a severe lack of expressiveness. Even if other projects, built from different premises, may be more successful, future research will center on these issues.

Continuity deserves the most attention at this juncture. "Eccentricities" may result when the ATN program shifts signatures and non-signatures into place without (currently) much regard for their potential connectivity. Non-linearity in general cannot help but create some problems. When composing linearly, one has the knowledge of events immediately preceding and following quite clearly in mind. When composing in the abstract, a section can have little reference to its ultimate neighbors. Refinements should be able to resolve at least some of these discontinuities.

Stylistic ambiguities may occur at least partially from the same source. Or it may be that the ambiguity is not in the EMI-produced examples but in the originals and we find the situation ambiguous because composers, unlike machines, do not so easily follow the rules we in hindsight give them. For example, the generic tonal music portion of this program worked for years creating four-bar phrase examples. When I finally figured out that only the worst of classical composers fit into this mold that we generally teach, the program developed significantly.

Finally, the lack of expressiveness presents three separate and very complicated problems. First, the machine compositions have little chance of obtaining the inspiration of great human composers. Perhaps, in its computer-assisted form, such inspiration may be injected into the ultimate composition. Otherwise, the aesthetic we believe purely human can only be obtained by the machine through refinements in pattern matching or similar sampling of actual works. The second problem, that of performance, can be addressed two ways: (1) through actual performance by humans or (2) through the creation of programs that can re-inject musical (not simply random) fluctuations into the tempo (particularly) of machine-composed works. Creation of such programs, even ones that imitate great performers by pattern matching their performances, will be a serious avenue for further research.

Most of the controversies surrounding computer composition seem to intensify in the context of popular music. For example, while programs such as EMI may further the career of one composer experiencing a block, might not it also put dozens of others out of work? Would it be in the best interests of a motion picture studio to purchase a computer program and avoid paying living composers salaries for new scores for its films?

But the hand of the composer is not absent from the finished product of computer-assisted composition. With experience it is possible that musicians and music lovers alike will "forgive" the machine and believe it to be a composer's tool in the same manner that a piano serves in improvisation. We may even come to understand that, as expressed in the previous paragraph, even purely machine-composed music is born of programs created by human inspiration.

BIBLIOGRAPHY

Cope, David. *Concert for Piano and Orchestra*. Greenville, Maine: Opus One Records, 82.

Fry, C. "Flavors Band: A Language for Specifying Musical Style." *Computer Music Journal* 8,4 (Winter 1984): 2–34.

Narmour, Eugene. *Beyond Schenkerism*. Chicago: University of Chicago Press, 1977.

Salzer, Felix. *Structural Hearing: Tonal Coherence in Music*. Vol. 2, New York: Dover Publications, 1962.

Winston, P. H. *Artificial Intelligence*. 2d. ed. Reading, Mass.: Addison-Wesley, 1984.

INDEX

· ·

239

stochastic music, 7, 8, 10–11, 12, 17. *See also* Xenakis, Iannis

Strange, Allen; *The Music of Dod*, 5

Stravinsky, Igor, 215–18

style dictionary, 89–92

sundari. *See* aeolian instruments

T

Tchaikowsky, Peter, 30

Tenney, James, 8; *Four Stochastic Studies*, 8; *Dialogue*, 8; *Stochastic String Quartet*, 8

texture, 48, 164; Bartók, Béla, and, 210; Brahms, Johannes, and, 204; *Concert for Piano and Orchestra* and, 229; counterpoint and, 48–50, 188; EMI and, 151–52, 154, 157; Mozart and, 33, 45, 147, 167; signatures and, 164; Xenakis, Iannis, and, 7

Theremin, Leon, 4

Thompson, James, 2

time-span reduction, 17

Todd, Peter, 16

tonic. *See* compose-invention variables

tonic-note. *See* compose-invention variables

top-down, 153; compositional approach, xiii, xv, 153; and language, 10; and music analysis, 43; programming

style, 38, 80–81; and Schenker's theories, 37

transformational grammars, xv, 10, 17, 18, 57, 61, 67

translate, 104–5, 107

transpose-second-voice, 132, 136

TREE, 12

Truax, Barry, 11

U

Ursatz, 37, 38. *See also* Schenker, Heinrich

V

variance. *See* compose-invention variables

Vercoe, Barry, 16

W

Webern, Anton von, 10

wind chimes. *See* aeolian instruments

Woods, William, 57

Wright, W., 7

X

Xenakis, Iannis, 7; *Achoripsis*, 7; *Metastasis*, 7; *Pithoprakta*, 7